PREACHING ON
FAVOURITE HYMNS

PREACHING ON FAVOURITE HYMNS

Sermon outlines on thirty-four selected hymns

Frank Colquhoun

Canon Emeritus of Norwich Cathedral

MOWBRAY
LONDON & OXFORD

ISBN 0 264 67054 X

First published 1986
by A.R. Mowbray & Co. Ltd,
Saint Thomas House, Becket Street,
Oxford, OX1 1SJ

Typeset by Comersgate Art Studios, Oxford
Printed in Great Britain by Biddles Ltd, Guildford

British Library Cataloguing in Publication Data

Colquhoun, Frank
    Preaching on favourite hymns: sermon outlines on
    thirty-four selected hymns. — (Mowbray's sermon outline
    series)
    1. Sermons — Outlines, syllabi, etc.
    I. Title
    251'.02   BV4223

ISBN 0-264-67054-X

CONTENTS

PREFACE

Throughout most of my ministry I have, from time to time, used a hymn as the basis of a sermon. I believe there is a value in this practice and that it is to be encouraged, for more than one reason.

To begin with, hymns have an important place in Christian worship and there is no doubt that people like singing them. But most congregations I fear know very little about them: their authorship and background, their contents and message. One purpose of the hymn-sermon is to remedy this state of affairs and help the congregation to sing their hymns with more interest and greater understanding.

Again, many hymns – especially those in the older tradition – are devotional treasures, rich in biblical language and allusions, and provide excellent material for sermons on various aspects of the spiritual life. When such hymns are sympathetically expounded from the pulpit the hungry sheep in the pews will not look up and remain hungry, though they may well hunger for more.

Thirdly, and closely related to this, is the fact that hymns have a considerable teaching value. This has long been recognized in the story of the Christian Church. It has often been suggested that church people learn more of their theology from the hymn book than from the Bible. At any rate, many popular hymns offer a ready-to-hand medium for teaching the cardinal truths of the Christian faith and for doing so in a form that people can readily grasp and possibly remember.

The handful of hymns I have chosen for this book represent a fairly wide variety of traditions and cover a good many themes. For the most part they are non-seasonal in character. I have indicated ways in which they may be introduced and presented in sermon form; but these are no more than suggestions. Clearly the same material may be arranged and presented in other ways. It is up to the preacher to select and adapt what is offered in whatever form he thinks best suited for the needs of his congregation.

No one preaching or writing on hymns in these days can fail to be indebted to the works of the late Dr Erik Routley (1917–82). The quotations in this book are from his *Hymns and the Faith*, 1955, by kind permission of John Murray (Publishers) Ltd.

I will only add that these notes may prove of interest to hymn lovers in general, and some may find them useful for personal meditation.

F.C.

1.

PRAISE

All people that on earth do dwell
(William Kethe, 16th c.)

This famous hymn has a particular claim on our attention. It is the earliest *English* hymn – that is, hymn written in the English language – still in general use today. It dates from 1560, three years after Queen Elizabeth came to the throne.

Properly speaking, of course, it is not a 'hymn' but a metrical psalm. It is the one hundredth psalm put into metre and rhyme. Let us take a look at it from three points of view.

1 A look at the background

For its origin we have to go back to the stormy days of the Reformation. During the reign of Queen Mary many English Protestants fled to the Continent to escape persecution. Among them was William Kethe, a clergyman of the English Church but probably a Scotsman by birth, who settled in Geneva. While there, he engaged in the task of translating the Bible into English; but he also had a hand in preparing a collection of metrical psalms, among which was this version of Psalm 100. The complete collection, known as the *Anglo-Genevan Psalter,* was published in 1561, both in Geneva and London.

At that time the English Church and all the Protestant bodies in Britain were committed to the Calvinistic tradition of singing only the biblical psalms in public worship. Unlike Luther, Calvin did not approve of hymns. We may well question his wisdom in this matter; but he was certainly right

1

in insisting that the whole congregation should have the privilege of joining in the praise of God and that they should do this in their own tongue, not in Latin as hitherto.

This then is the historical background of our hymn. We have little further knowledge of its author William Kethe. Even the dates of his birth and death are unrecorded. When later he left Geneva and returned to England he was chaplain to the forces under the Earl of Warwick and spent the last part of his life as rector of the Dorset village of Childe Okeford.

2 A look at the words

The hymn is derived wholly from Psalm 100. It is an amazingly skilful piece of paraphrasing. Equally noteworthy is the fact that its language has virtually remained unchanged since it was written more than four hundred years ago.

Two notes are dominant in the psalm. One is the note of *universality,* which rings out in the opening words: 'Make a joyful noise to the Lord, all the lands'. And the hymn echoes this:

> All people that on earth do dwell,
>   Sing to the Lord with cheerful voice.

All people! Jehovah is not only the God of the Jews. True, he revealed himself first to Israel, but he did so in order that *through* Israel he might reveal himself to all mankind. So the psalm invites people of every nation on earth to worship him. It is to *them* that the words are addressed: 'Enter his gates with thanksgiving and his courts with praise' (Ps.100). The psalmist envisages members of every race and nation surging through the temple gates in Jerusalem and crowding God's courts with songs of thanksgiving. This is how the hymn captures the picture

O enter then his gates with praise,
   Approach with joy his courts unto;
Praise, laud, and bless his name always,
   For it is seemly so to do.

There is no longer a court of the Gentiles. The temple has become, as God intended it to be, a house of prayer for all nations. Here is a glorious missionary vision.

Alongside its universality the psalm is marked by its *joyousness*. This note is heard in the opening words, and again in the second verse: 'Serve the Lord with gladness! Come into his presence with singing!' Kethe rendered this:

Him serve with fear, his praise forth tell,
   Come ye before him, and rejoice.

Clearly 'him serve with *fear*' is not satisfactory. The Lord is to be served with 'gladness'; so later the *Scottish Psalter* changed 'fear' to 'mirth' and several modern hymnals adopt this reading.

The secret of this joy is to acknowledge Jehovah as the only true God and be enrolled among his people (v.3 of the psalm). The hymn expresses it thus:

The Lord, ye know, is God indeed,
   Without our aid he did us make;
We are his folk, he doth us feed,
   And for his sheep he doth us take.

When the hymn was first published, the word *folk* was spelt in its Old English form of 'folck'. Not long afterwards this was thought to be a misprint for 'flock' and the line was changed accordingly. But this reading, which persisted for nearly three centuries, is clearly wrong. It does not correspond to the psalm which says 'We are his *people*' – that is, his folk. We are also his flock, as the last line says.

The final stanza gives the reason for our offering praise to

God. The expression 'For why' at the start simply means 'Because':

> For why, the Lord our God is good,
>   His mercy is for ever sure;
>   His truth at all times firmly stood,
>   And shall from age to age endure.

The Lord our God is good. Take those words to your heart and reflect on them. The Lord's goodness calls forth our highest praise. We never come to the end of it. What is more, as the hymn goes on to say, his *mercy* or loving-kindness endures for ever and his *truth* (or faithfulness, as the word means here) persists to all generations. Well may we sing the doxology that is sometimes added to the hymn.

3 A look at the tune

This famous hymn is wedded to an equally famous tune, the *Old Hundredth*, one of the finest of all psalm-tunes. The association dates back to 1561 and has remained unbroken ever since.

The tune was composed or adapted by Louis Bourgeois, a Frenchman who was born in Paris about 1510. He followed Calvin to Geneva, where he was appointed cantor of one of the churches and entrusted with the duty of providing music for the metrical psalter then in preparation. He was a dedicated and gifted musician and accomplished his task with distinction. Of the eighty-five tunes in the *Genevan Psalter*, published in 1551, a considerable number were his own. In that book this tune was set to a different psalm (Ps.134); but ten years later in the *Anglo-Genevan Psalter* it was attached to Kethe's version of Psalm 100, hence its title.

In all this we are reminded of the debt we owe to the musicians who have written the tunes for our hymns. Among them are some of the most eminent composers of olden and modern times. A hymn is essentially a thing to be sung: without a suitable tune it is nothing. So as we thank God for those who wrote the words of the hymns we sing, let us also thank him for those who composed the tunes – and did so, like the others, to the glory and praise of God.

2.

THE ETERNAL GOD

O God, our help in ages past
(Isaac Watts, 1674–1748)

The story is told that Dr Benjamin Jowett, Master of Balliol College, Oxford, once asked a company of dons to write down on a slip of paper a list of what they regarded as the finest English hymns. The result was surprising. Each of the lists contained only one hymn and in every case it was the same: 'O God, our help in ages past'.

It is unquestionably one of the greatest hymns in the English language. It comes into its own on big state occasions and has almost become a second national anthem. It was written by Isaac Watts, the father of English hymnody, as a free paraphrase of Psalm 90. Originally it began '*Our* God, our help . . .', but John Wesley changed the 'Our' to 'O' and most hymn books now adopt this. Of the nine stanzas Watts wrote, three have dropped out of use and the hymn is the better as well as the shorter for it. Its familiar tune *St Anne* was composed by William Croft, some time organist of St Anne's, Soho, and later of Westminster Abbey.

The hymn, like the psalm on which it is based, is about man and God, time and eternity, faith and fear.

1 Man and God

Watts entitled the hymn 'Man frail and God eternal'. This theme runs through all the stanzas. It also sums up the message of the psalm, which begins by focusing our gaze on the everlasting God, the creator of the world: 'Lord, thou hast been our dwelling place in all generations. Before the mountains were brought forth, or ever thou hadst formed the earth and the world, from everlasting to everlasting thou art God' (Ps.90.1,2). Watts reflects this thought in the words:

> Before the hills in order stood,
>   Or earth received her frame,
> From everlasting thou art God,
>   To endless years the same.

By contrast, the psalm next points to man and the transitory nature of human life: 'Thou turnest man back to the dust, and sayest, "Turn back, O children of men!" ' (Ps.90.3). In one of the stanzas missing from our books Watts matches this with the lines:

> Thy word commands our flesh to dust,
>   Return, ye sons of men;
> All nations rose from earth at first,
>   And turn to earth again.

Clearly enough, the reference is to the book of Genesis where it is said that God formed man from the dust of the ground, and after the Fall said to him, 'Dust thou art, and unto dust thou shalt return' (Gen. 2.7 and 3.19).

Man is frail, man is mortal. He is born only to die. The psalm likens his life to a passing dream and to the grass of the field which flourishes in the morning and in the evening withers away (Ps.90.5,6). No wonder the psalmist prays, 'So teach us to number our days, that we may apply our hearts unto wisdom' (Ps.90.12).

2 Time and eternity

It is well to be reminded of the brevity of our human life. And that life never appears too short as when measured against God's eternity. He is the everlasting God. He is raised above time. Time has no meaning for him. As the psalm says, 'A thousand years in thy sight are but as yesterday when it is past, or as a watch in the night' (Ps.90.4). Or, in the language of the hymn:

> A thousand ages in thy sight
> Are like an evening gone,
> Short as the watch that ends the night
> Before the rising sun.

Man on the other hand is a creature of time. 'For all our days pass away under thy wrath, our years come to an end like a sigh' (Ps.90.9). True, our years may be as many as seventy or eighty or even more; yet even so they are soon gone – and soon forgotten (Ps.90.10).

This is the truth that Isaac Watts is expressing in the stanza:

> Time, like an ever-rolling stream,
> Bears all its sons away;
> They fly forgotten, as a dream
> Dies at the opening day.

These words are often misunderstood and for that reason are sometimes not sung. This is especially the case at Remembrancetide. Is it true that our brave sons who have died for their country are quickly forgotten and fade from our memory as swiftly as a dream? Surely not! But that is not the meaning of Watts's lines. Look at them carefully and you will see that the 'sons' referred to are not *our* sons but the sons of *time*: a poetical figure denoting the days and weeks and years of the past. It is these that are so soon forgotten and pass into oblivion as new events take place and new tasks demand our attention.

In view of the shortness of life and the swift passage of time we may well echo another prayer to be found in this psalm: 'O satisfy us early with thy mercy, that we may rejoice and be glad all our days' (Ps.90.14).

3 Faith and fear

This hymn was written about the year 1714 when Britain was facing a political crisis. Queen Anne was nearing her end. She had no heir and there was widespread anxiety in the nation about the future, especially regarding the Protestant succession.

In such troubled times Watts wrote his famous lines in order to allay the people's fears and forebodings. From the very outset the hymn is a strong and vibrant affirmation of *faith*: faith in the eternal God and his sufficiency in every time of need:

> O God, our help in ages past,
>   Our hope for years to come,
> Our shelter from the stormy blast,
>   And our eternal home.

These words – which are virtually repeated in the final stanza – point us away from ourselves and our fears and fix our whole attention on *God*. They tell us what he is and what he means to those who put their trust in him.

God is our *help*. He has proved himself as such in ages past, in our own lives as well as in the life of our nation. As we look back over the years – many of them perilous and critical years – we can testify with confidence, 'Hitherto the Lord has helped us'.

For that very reason God is also our *hope* as we face the unknown future. The help he has already given in response to our prayers is the pledge and token that he will not fail us in the years to come. He is our faithful God, utterly dependable in every circumstance of life.

Finally, God is our *home*: that is, our spiritual abode, and as such 'our shelter from the stormy blast'. As the psalm declares, 'Lord, thou hast been our dwelling place in all generations' (Ps.90.1). Without him, we are homeless wanderers. In him, and in him alone, we 'rest secure'.

3.

PROVIDENCE

God moves in a mysterious way
(W. Cowper, 1731–1800)

This is beyond question the greatest hymn on the subject of divine providence. And only a man of William Cowper's poetical genius and spiritual insight could have written it. It was printed in the *Olney Hymns* (1779) under the heading, 'Light shining out of darkness'. It also had a text attached to it, the words of Jesus to Simon Peter at the feet-washing: 'What I do thou knowest not now, but thou shalt know hereafter.'

For a long time the story persisted that Cowper wrote the hymn just after he had mercifully been prevented from committing suicide. The story has no historical foundation and must be dismissed as a legend. The lines themselves are evidence that the hymn was written not in one of the poet's periods of darkness but in one of his most lucid moments.

As we look at it together we shall find that two contrasting notes run through the six stanzas. On the one hand, *perplexity* in face of life's strange and inexplicable happenings; on the other, *confidence* in God's wise and merciful ordering of our human affairs.

9

1 God's mysterious ways

The hymn begins with the acknowledgement that in his dealings with mankind God's ways *are* mysterious. This is an undeniable fact and we must accept it at the outset. Many of the things that happen in life – in our own lives and in the lives of others – are beyond our comprehension. We are baffled by them. They appear to be entirely irrational. Worst of all, they seem to be inconsistent with our belief as Christians in God's love and goodness. How can he allow such things to happen? We can only confess with St Paul, 'His judgements are unsearchable, his ways past finding out!' (Romans 11.33).

But at such times there is no cause for despondency, less still for despair. However dark the situation, God has not opted out of it. He is right in the middle of it – *and he is actively involved*. Note how Cowper boldly asserts that God *moves*. Mystery indeed there may well be but there is also movement. There is nothing static about divine providence. In ways beyond our understanding God is performing wonders:

> He plants his footsteps in the sea,
> And rides upon the storm.

This of course is poetic symbolism. We may take it that the *sea* here represents the perilous and unpredictable elements in life, while the *storm* refers to those turbulent, tempestuous events when things seem quite out of control. Yet God is there all the time. The sea is his highway, the storm is his chariot, and despite all appearances to the contrary he is actively at work:

> Deep in unfathomable mines
> Of never failing skill
> He treasures up his bright designs,
> And works his sovereign will.

Deep, *unfathomable*, hidden from our sight: such are the ways of God. But they are not haphazard. They follow a pattern –

'his bright designs' the poet calls what God is doing; and more important still, he is accomplishing 'his sovereign will'.

2 God's sovereign will

Note that phrase. In thinking of this subject of divine providence, how good it is to be reminded of the *sovereignty* of God. Come what may, the Lord reigneth! True, it doesn't always look as though he does. There are times when we are tempted to think that God has abdicated his throne and that the devil has taken over control. Or, maybe, we conclude that life has no meaning and that we are at the mercy of blind chance. What shall we say to that?

This is what Cowper says:

> Ye fearful saints, fresh courage take;
> The clouds ye so much dread
> Are big with mercy, and shall break
> In blessings on your head.

Fresh courage take! Certainly we need *courage* when things are desperately bad and we don't know what is going to happen next. But there is no need to be afraid. What we think are black thunder clouds that threaten to overwhelm us are no more than gracious rain clouds 'big with mercy', God's everlasting mercy; and when they break upon us they will shed showers of blessing.

Here we are at the heart of the hymn's message. In God's gracious providence light does shine out of darkness, good comes out of evil, tribulations are turned into bllesings. Not all at once, in all likelihood, but in the final outworking of God's sovereign will. Just as his ways are not our ways, his times are not our times. So we are driven back, as the poet was, to the words of Jesus: 'What I am doing you do not know *now*, but afterwards you will understand.' In the meantime we must be patient while God works out his bright designs, his purposes of

love. And we shall not have to wait for ever, for another verse
says:

> His purposes will ripen fast,
> Unfolding every hour;
> The bud may have a bitter taste,
> But sweet will be the flower.

Here once again we have the language of poetic symbolism.
Cowper draws an illustration from the world of nature, the bud
and the flower. There is nothing particularly attractive about
the bud; yet the bud must come before the flower, for the
flower emerges from the bud. And when it does emerge in all its
loveliness of form and colour there is a complete transforma-
tion. So it is with ourselves. For a while things in our lives may
have an ugly look and we harbour bitter feelings; but in course
of time, with the flowering of God's purpose, we see everything
in a different light. The fact is, life does not yield its true
meaning all at once. In facing life's dark mysteries we certainly
need *patience* as well as courage.

3 Faith, not reason

And we need something else besides – and that is *faith*. So
Cowper admonishes us:

> Judge not the Lord by feeble sense,
> But trust him for his grace;
> Behind a frowning providence
> He hides a smiling face.

The reason why we may and should trust God is because of
his *grace*: his free, boundless, unmerited love for us sinners.
Such is the smiling face of God, revealed to us in Jesus Christ,
that lies behind what may appear to be a frowning providence.

All too readily we may misjudge the ways of God, especially
if we depend simply on our 'feeble sense', that is, our own

unaided reason. We shall find little comfort or help in that direction. Reason alone does not get us very far in grappling with the mystery of providence. Not that faith is opposed to reason. Rather faith transcends reason and rises to a higher level, the spiritual level. Faith is perceptive of the things of God, whereas, as the final stanza says,

> Blind unbelief is sure to err,
>   And scan his works in vain;
> God is his own interpreter,
>   And he will make it plain.

God does many things that we do not and cannot understand *at the present*. We are circumscribed by time. The future is veiled from our eyes. But not from God's. He sees the end from the beginning. He knows what he is about and we can trust him fully. He is his own interpreter and in his own time he will make everything clear. So with confidence we can say with St Paul, 'We know that in all things God works for the good of those who love him, who have been called according to his purpose' (Romans 8.28).

4.

JACOB'S DREAM

Nearer, my God, to thee
(Sarah F. Adams, 1805–48)

Sarah Flower Adams (her married name) was a Unitarian. This hymn and a dozen others were written for a hymn book published in 1841 for use in the Unitarian chapel in London to which she and her husband belonged. She possessed a genuine gift of poetry and her work was admired by Robert Browning; but nearly all she wrote has now been forgotten apart from this hymn. The story persists that it was sung on that terrible night in 1912 when the *Titanic* sank in the north Atlantic with the loss of over 1,600 lives. The dance band, so it is said, assembled on deck and played the hymn as the giant liner sank beneath the icy waters. The story has never been fully verified. It may be purely legendary but quite likely it embodies an element of truth.

When the hymn first appeared it met with a lot of criticism. The literary-minded pointed out that it is really a poem, not a hymn suited for public worship. Some orthodox Christians rejected it out of hand because of its Unitarian authorship. Yet others dismissed it because it lacks any mention of Christ. But this latter criticism carries no weight. The same charge could be levelled just as truly against many famous hymns, especially those which are metrical versions of the Jewish psalms. For example, 'The Lord's my shepherd' (Psalm 23) or 'Praise, my soul, the King of heaven' (Psalm 103). Sarah Adams' verses fall into the same category. They are firmly biblical in character and are based on a well-known Old Testament story.

1 God's mercy

The story is that of Jacob's dream (Genesis 28.11–19) and is a record of God's mercy. At the time the patriarch was in dire trouble. He had grievously wronged his brother Esau and robbed him of his birthright. Now he was a fugitive, seeking refuge from his brother's wrath. He was a lonely, homeless and frightened man. And in the strange land to which he had fled he believed that God, the God of his fathers, had abandoned him.

Then it was that he had his remarkable dream. With a stone for a pillow he laid down to sleep . . .

And he dreamed that there was a ladder set up on the earth and the top of it reached to heaven; and behold, the angels of God were ascending and descending on it! And behold, the Lord stood above it and said, 'I am the Lord, the God of Abraham your father and the God of Isaac; the land on which you lie I will give to you and to your descendants . . . . And behold, I am with you and will keep you wherever you go, and I will bring you back to this land . . . .

The dream was a revelation of divine grace. Jacob had mistakenly thought that, far from home, he was also far from God. But the ladder he saw reaching from earth to heaven, with celestial messengers ascending and descending it, taught him that after all God was not far off, nor in that strange land was he inaccessible. 'Surely the Lord is in this place and I did not know it!' he cried on waking. 'This is none other than the house of God and this is the gate of heaven!'

Bethel, the name he gave to the place where this happened, means 'the house of God'. There he discovered to his astonishment that, wander where he might, God was still with him, near at hand, nearer than he had realized before.

In her hymn Sarah Adams puts the story and its meaning into poetry:

> Though, like the wanderer,
>   The sun gone down,
> Darkness be over me,
>   My rest a stone;
> Yet in my dreams I'd be
> Nearer, my God, to thee,
>   Nearer to thee.
>
> There let the way appear,
>   Steps unto heaven;
> All that thou sendest me
>   In mercy given:

15

> Angels to beckon me
> Nearer, my God, to thee,
> Nearer to thee.

Nearer to thee! The refrain occurs twelve times in the complete five stanzas. It is the hymn's dominant theme and that theme is developed along two contrasting lines.

2 Earth's sorrows

First, and most emphatically, the hymn develops the idea that earth's sorrows, our troubles and trials, far from separating us from God may be steps on a ladder lifting us closer to him. This thought is expressed in the opening words:

> Nearer, my God, to thee,
> Nearer to thee,
> E'en though it be a cross
> That raiseth me.

The *cross* here is not the cross on which Jesus died for our sins. The word is used as a symbol of suffering and trial. Mrs Adams knew something of what that meant in her later life. As a young woman her ambition had been to go on the stage. After her marriage at the age of twenty-nine her husband encouraged her to do this. A year or two later she successfully played Lady Macbeth in a London theatre. It seemed that she was on the brink of a brilliant career as an actress. But the strain proved too great and soon afterwards her health completely broke down. She was forbidden to act again, to her great disappointment. She never fully recovered and died of tuberculosis at the age of forty-three.

It may well be that the hymn reflects her experience of grief and suffering. But she refused to be discouraged by the things that had happened or allow them to destroy her faith. She learned from the story of Jacob's dream that faith can triumph over trouble and that it is possible to know God's nearness when things are at their worst. St Paul spoke of being 'joyful in tribulation' and this finds an echo in the fourth stanza:

> Then, with my waking thoughts,
>   Bright with thy praise,
> Out of my stony griefs
>   Bethel I'll raise;
> So by my woes to be
> Nearer, my God, to thee,
>   Nearer to thee.

The 'stony griefs' refers to the stone which the patriarch used for a pillow and which in the morning he set up and consecrated as a memorial to God's mercy. Someone remarked that it is worth having a hard pillow if it brings us visions of God. Our 'woes' may be a means of drawing us nearer to him, if we learn to accept them and not turn bitter.

3 Life's joys

But there is another aspect of this subject. It is not only our troubles and woes that can bring us nearer to God. Life's joys and blessings may and should do the same. Sarah Adams recognized this when, forsaking the Bible story, she added a fifth stanza to her hymn:

> Or, if on joyful wing
>   Cleaving the sky,
> Sun, moon, and stars forgot,
>   Upwards I fly,
> Still all my song shall be,
> Nearer, my God, to thee,
>   Nearer to thee.

Many hymn books omit this verse. This is plainly a mistake, for without it the hymn presents a false and unbalanced picture of life. As Sarah Adams' friend, Robert Browning, observed, we should not view the world as a vale of tears. There are indeed many disappointments and trials to be encountered in the world. Most of us can verify that fact. Nevertheless God's goodness and mercy still follow us all our days and lift us up to him on wings of joy and praise and thanksgiving.

5.

THE SHEPHERD PSALM

The Lord's my Shepherd, I'll not want
(Scottish Psalter, 1650)

From the very beginning the Christian Church has been a singing Church, as the New Testament makes clear. It also makes clear that from the beginning the psalms of the Old Testament have had an important place in its worship; and of those psalms none is more popular or more precious than the beautiful shepherd psalm, Psalm 23. Our hymn is the metrical version of that psalm from the *Scottish Psalter* of 1650. Queen Elizabeth chose it for her marriage service in Westminster Abbey in 1947, sung to the tune *Crimond*, and that at once made both words and music widely known.

The words are of mixed authorship. No single name can be attached to them. But we are better off when it comes to the tune, which is of later date. It was the work of Miss Jessie Irvine (1836–87), whose father was for many years minister of the church at Crimond in Aberdeenshire. It has become the generally accepted melody for the words, though others (like *Brother James's Air*) are still in use.

18

In origin this is of course a Jewish song, but it is full of Christian meaning. This is because when we sing its opening line we instinctively think of the Lord Jesus who said, 'I am the good shepherd; the good shepherd lays down his life for his sheep'.

The hymn begins with a strong, personal affirmation of faith, 'The Lord's my shepherd', and everything else follows from that. For if the Lord is my shepherd I can also say 'I'll not want'. The shepherd takes care of our 'wants' – that is of the things we lack – and the rest of the psalm tells us what they are.

1 Rest and peace

One thing we shall not 'want' is inward peace.

> The Lord's my shepherd, I'll not want;
> He makes me down to lie
> In pastures green; he leadeth me
> The quiet waters by.

The language, like a lot of the Bible language, is pictorial; and the picture here is perfectly clear. It is a very restful scene. You can see it in your mind's eye: the 'pastures green' basking in the sunshine, and in a shady corner of the meadow 'the quiet waters' of a pond. It is a picture of peace. And peace is what we all long for and desperately need. For after all, what is life worth without peace – peace of heart, peace of mind, peace of conscience?

People are grasping after more and more money, as though that were what matters most in life. It is a delusion and a lie. There are a lot of things that money can buy, but inward peace is not one of them. Such peace is worth more than all the money in the world. It is the Lord's gift to those who trust in him.

2 Restoration and guidance

The psalm goes on to speak of how the Lord restores and guides us:

> My soul he doth restore again,
>   And me to walk doth make
> Within the paths of righteousness,
>   E'en for his own name's sake.

Restoration. The picture of the shepherd and the sheep is still in mind. Sheep sometimes go astray. We know that; and *we* do the same. In the words of the old Prayer Book confession, 'We have erred and strayed from thy ways like lost sheep'. That is true of us all, whether we admit it or not. But the wonder of God's love is that when in our folly we wander from him, he seeks us and finds us – and restores us to himself. Jesus' parable of the lost sheep perfectly illustrates this (Luke 15).

And then the shepherd *guides* us. He leads us 'within the paths of righteousness'. That is *where* he guides us, in the right paths, right in his sight. And next is *why* he guides us, 'e'en for his own name's sake'. God's name is love, and because he loves us so much he doesn't want us to miss the way in life.

3 Companionship and comfort

With the next stanza the scene changes. Up to this point it has been all sunshine, but now the shadows gather. We are passing through a valley of deep darkness: 'death's dark vale', as the hymn puts it. Most of us know something about that.

> Yea, though I walk in death's dark vale,
>   Yet will I fear no ill;
> For thou art with me, and thy rod
>   And staff me comfort still.

There *are* dark valleys in life. The sun does not always shine for the believer and the Bible does not promise that it will. The darkness may be that of death, or it may take some other form: illness, sorrow, anxiety, disappointment, loneliness. These things are part of the pattern of life for many. Can our faith help us then?

Yes, for the mercy is that we don't have to tread the dark valley alone. The shepherd is by our side: 'thou art with me'. Note the *'thou'*. Before it was 'he'; now it is 'thou'. As the American evangelist D. L. Moody used to say, you may talk *about* the shepherd, but when you get into the dark valley you will talk *to* him. His rod and staff give us comfort, the psalm says. True; but our greatest comfort is the shepherd's own unfailing presence which dispels every fear.

4 Grace and glory

Towards the end the psalm takes another turn. The shepherd becomes the *host* and now we are invited to a banquet.

> My table thou hast furnished
> In presence of my foes;
> My head thou dost with oil anoint,
> And my cup overflows.

Feasting and fighting! Such is the picture we are given here of the Christian life. It is true that as long as life lasts we are in the presence of our foes: the world, the flesh, and the devil. And they will never leave us alone. But this also is true, that as long as life lasts the Lord's table will always be spread and richly furnished. This is the symbol of his abundant grace – not only sufficient but more than sufficient, so that we can sing 'And my cup overflows'. If our cup does indeed run over (as the AV puts it) let us pray that others may benefit from the overflow.

The hymn's final stanza surveys life's prospects. First:

> Goodness and mercy all my life
> Shall surely follow me.

21

This is the immediate outlook – God's goodness and mercy through all our remaining days. And when those days come to an end, the outlook is even brighter:

> And in God's house for evermore
> My dwelling-place shall be.

What a prospect! Grace now and glory hereafter. This psalm begins on earth and ends in heaven. It begins in time and ends in eternity. It begins with an affirmation of faith, 'The Lord is my shepherd'; it ends with an assurance of hope: 'I will dwell in the house of the Lord for ever'.

6.

A SONG OF DELIVERANCE

Through all the changing scenes of life
(New Version of the Psalms, 1696)

One of the many blessings of the Reformation was the restoring of hymn-singing to the common worship of the Church. In the Middle Ages hymns were virtually confined to the monasteries, where they were sung (in Latin, of course) in the round of the daily services. The reformers made it their business to change this by providing hymns in the language of the people for congregational use.

Martin Luther led the way in Germany. He himself wrote hymns – and encouraged others to do the same – as a means of teaching the reformed faith. But Calvin, the French reformer, sensed a danger here. He feared that hymns, as purely human compositions, might contain false teaching. He therefore insisted that only metrical *psalms* should be sung in church worship: that is, the biblical psalms turned into verse.

It was this tradition that prevailed in England and Scotland. In the English Church a complete metrical psalter was published shortly after Queen Elizabeth I came to the throne. This later became known as the *Old Version*. It was miserably poor poetry and was eventually succeeded, in 1696, by the much improved *New Version* of Tate and Brady. Both these were Irish clergymen, Nahum Tate being the Poet Laureate and Nicholas Brady chaplain to King William. From this freer and more poetical rendering of the psalms two have survived in shortened forms: 'As pants the hart for cooling streams'(Ps.42) and 'Through all the changing scenes of life' (Ps.34).

This is the hymn we now look at. As we do so let us note how the Bible text of the psalm (roughly the first nine verses) has been turned into the poetry of the hymn in what is the finest example of Tate and Brady's work.

1 The note of praise

The psalm begins on the note of praise: 'I will bless the Lord at all times; his praise shall continually be in my mouth.' This is taken up in the hymn:

> Through all the changing scenes of life,
> In trouble and in joy,
> The praises of my God shall still
> My heart and tongue employ.

You can see at once that this is a paraphrase rather than a literal rendering of the psalm. The short phrase 'at all times' is expanded into 'Through all the changing scenes of life, in trouble and in joy'. It makes good poetry as well as good sense. Life's scenes and circumstances are constantly changing with the passage of time. We have our good days and our bad ones, and our fluctuating moods reflect that fact. But our praise of

23

God should not be of the same variable character. To praise God is our first and constant duty and there is no time when it should be withheld. 'Joyful in tribulation' is the Bible maxim.

The psalm goes on (Ps.34.3,4): 'O magnify the Lord with me, and let us exalt his name together! I sought the Lord and he answered me, and delivered me from all my fears.' This is splendidly rendered:

> O magnify the Lord with me,
>   With me exalt his name;
> When in distress to him I called,
>   He to my rescue came.

The psalmist wasn't content to praise God on his own. He invited others to join with him in a partnership of praise. God had graciously answered his prayer. Let everyone know about it and glorify the Lord with him. Let us magnify his name *together!*

2 *The voice of testimony*

The note of praise is thus blended with the voice of testimony. Further testimony follows as the hymn takes up another verse of the psalm: 'The angel of the Lord encamps round those who fear him, and delivers them' (Ps.34.7). Hence:

> The hosts of God encamp around
>   The dwellings of the just;
> Deliverance he affords to all
>   Who on his succour trust.

Note the word *deliverance*. It is one of the leading ideas of the psalm. In one form or another the verb to 'deliver' occurs several times. One of the reasons why the writer was so filled with praise was because God had mercifully delivered him when his life was in danger. (Note: the Bible heading of the psalm identifies the occasion: see 1 Samuel 21.10ff.)

The psalm speaks of the deliverance being wrought by 'the angel of the Lord'. This is a term often used for the presence of God himself. In the hymn another phrase is used: 'the hosts of God'. But the ultimate meaning is the same. The psalmist is testifying to the fact that God guards and preserves the lives of those who fear him.

Can we be sure of that? Will he do the same for us? The answer given in the psalm is: 'O taste and see that the Lord is good! Happy is the man who takes refuge in him!' (Ps.34.8). This becomes in the hymn:

> O make but trial of his love;
> Experience will decide
> How blest they are, and only they,
> Who in his truth confide.

'Taste and see', says the psalm. 'Experience will decide', says the hymn. This is what Christians of earlier generations called experimental religion: that is, religion tested by first-hand experience. It is the practical, commonsense approach. If you want to know if an apple is good to eat, you don't argue about it. You taste and see. And if you want to know whether the religion of Jesus Christ is true or not, the best thing is to take the step of faith and try it for yourself. The truth of the gospel cannot be demonstrated on rational grounds alone. It vindicates itself in the hearts and lives of God's believing people.

3 The word of challenge

Testimony is followed by challenge in the hymn's final stanza:

> Fear him, ye saints, and you will then
> Have nothing else to fear;
> Make you his service your delight,
> Your wants shall be his care.

This is the rendering of the words in the psalm, 'O fear the

25

Lord, you his saints, for those who fear him have no want' (v.9). The fear of the Lord is a favourite Old Testament expression. It is that holy fear which includes the elements of reverence, obedience, trust, and worship. And the hymn rightly says that those who thus fear the Lord 'have nothing else to fear' – yes, and *no one* else to fear either. The challenge is clear: to fear God alone. It was said of John Knox, the Scottish reformer, that he feared man so little because he feared God so much.

Something else. To walk in the fear of the Lord is to be free from anxiety. For there is another challenge here: 'Make you his service your delight'. And if we do that, what then? 'Your wants shall be his care.' Note the balance between the two sentences. *We* make *his* service *our* delight. *He* makes *our* wants *his* care.

We have a faithful, merciful and generous Father who not only knows all about our needs but provides for them as he sees best. As another verse of the psalm says, 'The young lions suffer want and hunger; but those who seek the Lord lack no good thing' (Ps.34.10).

7.

JESU, DULCIS MEMORIA

Jesu, the very thought of thee
(c. 12th cent. Tr. E. Caswall, 1814–78)

This hymn is part of a long Latin poem dating back to the Middle Ages. Until fairly recent times its authorship was always ascribed to St Bernard (1091–1153), the famous abbot of Clairvaux in France, a man renowned for his sanctity and simplicity of life. But researches carried out by scholars in the present century seriously question this tradition. One important face that has come to light is that the earliest texts were copied in *England* and that from England they passed to France – not vice versa. Hence it is now concluded that the hymn was the work of an Englishman and that it was written about the end of the twelfth century. The unknown author was probably, like Bernard, a Cistercian monk. His verses certainly incorporate some phrases from Bernard's well known writings, and this explains no doubt why the work was formerly ascribed to him.

The hymn we now sing consists of fragments from the original poem, translated by the Roman Catholic scholar Edward Caswall. Another translation is that by the Anglican James Mason Neale, beginning 'Jesu, the very thought is sweet'. The hymn is wholly devotional in character and lends itself admirably to quiet reflection and meditation. Let us see what we can gather from it.

1 The name of Jesus

The hymn's dominant theme is the name of *Jesus*: the name given to him before his birth by the angel who appeared to Joseph. Jesus is the Greek form of the Hebrew *Joshua* and means 'saviour'. It is therefore the name of our salvation and is the dearest of all names, as the Church has always recognized. In the fifteenth century it was decided to set apart a special day in celebration of the name. Under pressure from the Franciscans the Pope authorized the feast of the Name of Jesus to be observed on 14 January. This hymn became the office hymn for the feast. In England the date was later changed to 7 August, as in the calendar of the 1662 Prayer Book. The feast has been dropped from the revised calendar (1980), and perhaps this is wise. For the name of Jesus is to be venerated

27

and adored not on one day of the year but every day. And what a name it is!

> No voice can sing, no heart can frame,
>   Nor can the memory find
> A sweeter sound than thy blest name,
>   O Saviour of mankind!

Note how in these lines four of our faculties are called into use in relation to the sacred name: our *memories* to recall it, our *hearts* to treasure it, our *voices* to sing it, our *ears* to hear it. Perhaps we should say not 'it' but 'him', for the name is the *person* – Jesus himself, the 'Saviour of mankind'.

2 The love of Jesus

Jesus is our Saviour because of his *love* for us: the love he demonstrated when he died on the cross, the love that he now exhibits in his gracious dealings with us.

> To those who fall, how kind thou art,
>   How good to those who seek!
>
> But what to those who find? Ah, this
>   Nor tongue nor pen can show;
> The love of Jesus, what it is,
>   None but his loved ones know.

Seeking and finding: two stages in the believer's quest for Jesus and an echo of his own promise, 'Seek, and you will find'. A point of particular interest is that in this hymn the unknown writer is quoting some words of St Bernard: 'How good thou art to the soul that seeks! But what to him who finds?' The answer given to that question is that it is unanswerable! No human words can express the love of Jesus. It is immeasurable. Yet paradoxically the apostle prays that we may *know* that love even though it passes knowledge (Ephesians 3.19). For while it is beyond our intellectual grasp, it is not beyond our spiritual apprehension. What words cannot express the heart can experience.

This is the meaning of the lines which state that 'none but his loved ones know' what the love of Jesus is. That of course is perfectly true; but it is actually a mistranslation. The Latin text refers not to Jesus' 'loved ones' – that is, those whom *he* loves – but to those who love *him*. It seems that the translator hesitated to write, as he should have done, 'None but his *lovers* know'. Yet that is the correct rendering and it makes a significant difference. We are *all* Christ's loved ones, however unworthy. But it is only those who love him in return that are able to comprehend something of the wonder and wealth of his love and what it means to them.

3 The presence of Jesus

There is one other theme in the hymn that invites our attention and that is the *presence* of Jesus. The opening verse makes reference to this. The very thought of Jesus is sweet,

> But sweeter far thy face to see,
> And in thy presence rest.

To think of Jesus is good. To catch a glimpse of him by faith is better. To find rest in his presence is best of all.

How do we enjoy the saviour's presence? In answering that question we must remember that he is in fact *always* present with us; but we on our part are not always aware of it. To *enjoy* his presence we must live close to him, keep in touch with him, never lose sight of him. The hymn as a whole implies this kind of intimacy with our Lord; and as that becomes increasingly a reality in our lives we shall discover more and more what he can mean to us.

The final stanza tells us something of that in the form of a prayer:

Jesu, our only joy be thou,
  As thou our prize wilt be;
Jesu, be all our glory now,
  And through eternity.

Once again we have a triplicate of thoughts. What is Jesus to us? He is our *joy* in this present life; he will be our *prize* in the life to come; and both now and then he is our *glory*.

Though not written by St Bernard, this hymn certainly reflects his spirit and in particular his deep, personal devotion to our Lord. In his writings he made extensive use of the Bible – 'not so much,' as he said, 'in order to expound the words as to reach the people's hearts'. This hymn, surely, does that too. It reaches the heart. And that is where all true religion begins.

8.

ADORATION

King of glory, King of peace
(George Herbert, 1593–1633)

George Herbert, the seventeenth century country parson, has become a legendary figure in the story of the English Church. A man of saintly character, and exemplary in his home and family life, he was a model of what a parish priest should be. His name now fittingly finds a place in the Church calendar of the *ASB* (27 February).

Herbert was also one of the leading poets of his day and it is by his verse that he is now chiefly remembered. He belonged to a group known as the metaphysical poets and this explains why his language is not always easy to understand. It is often

quaint and epigrammatic, sometimes elusive and obscure; but
it has great charm and it is well worthwhile seeking out its
hidden meaning.

'King of glory, King of peace' provides a good example of
this aspect of his work. It was published with all his other
poems in a book called *The Temple* a year after his death and
headed simply 'Praise'. Brief though that title is, it provides the
key to the poem. Praise – that is, the praise of God – is its
dominant theme. From it we can learn something about the
ministry of praise, both in relation to our worship and to our
lives.

1 Praise: the expression of love

One thing we learn is that praise is the expression of our love
for God. It is the language of the heart's peace:

> King of glory, King of peace,
>   I will love thee;
> And that love may never cease,
>   I will move thee.

'I will love thee', says the poet. To love God is the first and
greatest commandment. We are given the power to love in
order that we may love God. Another word for such love is
adoration; and adoration is of the very essence of worship. It is
indeed the highest and purest form of worship because it is the
most selfless. In such adoring praise we forget ourselves and
give to the Lord the honour due to his name. We also
acknowledge his sovereignty, as does George Herbert when he
addresses God as 'King of glory, King of peace'. In his earlier
life he had served at the court of James I, and it seems that he
instinctively thinks of God in his divine majesty. So should we.
In doing so we offer him our homage as well as our devotion.

To put adoration at the centre of worship is to prevent it
from becoming unduly subjective and sentimental. *God* must

31

dominate our worship, not we ourselves. We must look *up* and not keep looking within. Of course, we do not forget that we are sinners and in another part of the hymn we acknowledge that fact:

> Though my sins against me cried,
> Thou didst clear me.

We come together in worship as sinners whom God has 'cleared', that is, accepted and forgiven; and as a result we are now *free* – free from the bondage of self and sin, free to pour out our love to God in praise because of his infinite love for us.

2 *Praise: in music and song*

Another thing we learn is that our praise of God in public worship is offered through the medium of music and song. It is to this that the poet refers in the lines:

> Wherefore with my utmost art
> I will sing thee,
> And the cream of all my heart
> I will bring thee.

By his 'utmost art' Herbert doubtless means the art of music. He himself was a highly gifted musician. He greatly loved music and twice a week he walked from his country parish to Salisbury to hear the music in the cathedral.

It can be argued, of course, that music is not essential to worship; but it is virtually essential to *public* worship. The easiest way for a congregation to unite in common praise is by singing together. For all practical purposes worship and song are inseparable. But note: George Herbert declared not only that he would sing to God with the aid of music but that he would also bring 'the cream' of all his heart – that is, the riches of his heart's devotion.

We must remember that he was a poet, not a hymn-writer.

In his time hymns, as distinct from metrical psalms, were unknown in church worship. But he would surely have rejoiced had he known that centuries later several of his poems would become part of the Church's hymnody, matched to fine melodies to make an offering of praise to God.

3 Praise: a daily offering

We learn a final lesson from this hymn. Our praise of God is not simply a Sunday occupation:

> Seven whole days, not one in seven,
>> I will praise thee;
> In my heart, though not in heaven,
>> I can raise thee.

We must praise God not once a week when we go to church, but every day we live. How can we do that? 'In my heart', says the poet – a second reference to the fact that the heart of praise is the praise of the heart.

But as a good parish priest Herbert fully recognized the value of corporate and vocal worship, and in his village he *daily* conducted morning and evening prayer. His biographer, Izaak Walton, says that these services were attended not only by the neighbouring gentry but by the village folk and farm workers as well. 'They did so reverence Mr Herbert that they would let their plough rest when his bell rang to prayers, that they might offer their devotions to God with him, and then return to the plough.'

We live in very different times today; but the fact remains that whether in public worship or in the quietness of our hearts we must daily offer up our praises with our prayers to God. But it does not end here. It will have its consummation in heaven. Yet

> E'en eternity's too short
> To extol thee

This is a fine poetical note on which to end. But it suggests a practical reflection. If indeed an eternity of praise awaits us in heaven, ought we not to get into practice now?

9.

LOVE UNKNOWN

My song is love unknown
(S. Crossman, 1624–84)

Samuel Crossman, the man who wrote this hymn and who at the end of his life became Dean of Bristol Cathedral, died in 1684. This means that the hymn was written over three hundred years ago. Yet for two hundred years it was virtually lost sight of, till in 1868 it appeared in an obscure Victorian hymnal. Another fifty years and more were to pass before it became widely known with the publication of *Songs of Praise* in 1925. In that book it was set to a new tune, specially written for it by John Ireland, a foremost English composer renowned as a writer of songs. His tune, *Love Unknown*, almost at once popularized the hymn. It not only perfectly matches the words but has the effect of heightening their meaning.

What then is the meaning of this fine seventeenth century hymn and how are we to regard it? It is in part a narrative poem, relating in pictorial language the story of Jesus from his birth to his death. But the particular emphasis is upon the events of Holy Week, so that it is essentially a Passiontide hymn. And dominating the work as a whole is the majestic theme of the love of Christ, the note on which it both begins and ends.

1 Love incarnate

The opening words provide the key to the hymn:

> My song is love unknown,
>   My Saviour's love to me,
> Love to the loveless shown,
>   That they might lovely be.

This is a love song, a song about 'love unknown': unknown
in the twofold sense that it is all too little known and that it
surpasses human knowledge (Ephesians 3.19). No one can
measure its breadth and length, its height and depth. It is
infinite. Yet this love of the Saviour for the sinner is not a
'mystery', something far beyond our grasp. It has been manif-
ested and demonstrated in the Jesus of history. It is love
incarnate, love enfleshed in a human body. It is 'love to the
loveless shown' – and shown supremely in the cross.

This is where *we* come in. For the wonderful thing is that the
love of Jesus is not simply love for mankind in general. It is
love for each one of us personally, so that we can say,

> O who am I,
>   That for my sake
>   My Lord should take
> Frail flesh, and die?

Who am I? An unworthy sinner? Yes! But a worthless one?
No! Look at the question in the light of the cross and you will
see the difference that makes. We have been bought at a price.
We are precious to God. The life of every one of us is invested
with a new value because of the love that was not only made
flesh for us at Bethlehem but also made sin for us at Calvary.

2 Love rejected

What happened when Jesus took our human nature and lived

35

among us? The words of St John's Gospel supply the answer: 'He came to his own; that is, his own world, his own realm,' and those who were his own; his own people, 'would not receive him'. They refused to own him as the long promised Christ. He was not the sort of Messiah they expected, a mighty warrior-king who would make war upon their enemies. Nor was his the salvation they wanted, an earthly empire no longer subject to the Roman power. In effect they said, 'We will not have this man to reign over us' – and they rejected his love.

That rejection reached its climax with the events of the last great week, beginning with Palm Sunday:

> Sometimes they strew his way,
>   And his sweet praises sing,
> Resounding all the day
>   Hosannas to their King.
>
> Then 'Crucify!'
>   Is all their breath,
>   And for his death
> They thirst and cry.

The next stanza opens with the question, 'Why, what hath my Lord done?' – meaning, *Why* did the people thirst and cry for his death? If a man is reckoned worthy to die he must have done something to deserve it. In the case of Jesus, what *had* he done? Nothing but good. What deeds had he committed? None but works of mercy. 'He made the lame to run, he gave the blind their sight.' Were those his offences? Was it for such 'injuries' that his people spurned him? In thus condemning him his enemies condemned themselves.

3 Love victorious

The hymn considers a further aspect of the passion story. In what spirit did Jesus meet the rage and spite of his foes?

They rise, and needs will have
   My dear Lord made away;
A murderer they save,
   The Prince of Life they slay.
     Yet cheerful he
      To suffering goes,
     That he his foes
From thence might free.

Love is rejected, but love is not defeated. In the bitter conflict of that first Good Friday the victory was not with the religious authorities or the Roman power. True, his enemies had their way in the end and slew the prince of life. They showed their estimate of him by choosing the murderer Barabbas to be released rather than he, the sinless one. It seemed that evil was in complete control that day.

But no! Jesus was victor throughout. He was in perfect command of himself. He faced his accusers with dignified silence. He did not retaliate. He did not flinch or falter. He went forward to his suffering calm, courageous, fearless, resolute. The hymn uses the word 'cheerful'. For the joy that was set before him he endured the cross. The crucified Christ is the victorious Christ. His unconquerable love vanquished evil, redeemed mankind, and opened athe kingdom of heaven to all believers.

4 Love adored

The hymn ends on the note of adoration, with a song of praise.

Here might I stay and sing,
   No story so divine;
Never was love, dear King,
   Never was grief like thine.

'Here might I stay *and sing.*' Note those last two words. If in imagination we linger for a while at the cross of Jesus it is not to mourn for him, as though he were dead. It is to sing of him, it is to worship him. For he is the living Lord who both died *and* rose again. This is the gospel story, the 'story so divine'. It is the story of the Saviour's matchless love and what that love achieved for each of us. And it is this that calls forth our love and praise

> This is my Friend,
>   In whose sweet praise
>   I all my days
> Could gladly spend.

A final suggestion. Sometime, in a quiet moment, look back over the verses and note the titles given to Jesus. At the beginning he is addressed as 'my Saviour'; four times he is called 'my Lord'; twice 'my Friend', and once 'dear King'. Dwell on those titles and ask yourself, Is this what Jesus is to me? If not, why not? If so, am I praising him all my days?

10.

THE WONDROUS CROSS

When I survey the wondrous cross
(Isaac Watts, 1674–1748)

Matthew Arnold, shortly before he died, remarked that this was the finest hymn in the English language. It is almost certainly the finest of the six hundred or so hymns written by the great Dr Isaac Watts. He published it in 1707 in his *Hymns and Spiritual Songs* and placed it among the hymns for the Lord's Supper. But, while it is a splendid communion hymn, it makes no direct reference to the sacrament and serves a far wider purpose. Watts entitled it, 'Crucifixion to the world by the Cross of Christ', and attached to it the text: 'God forbid that I should glory, save in the cross of our Lord Jesus Christ, by whom the world is crucified to me, and I to the world' (Galatians 6.14).

The hymn invites us to look at the cross: not simply to give it a hasty and casual glance but to *survey* it. That long, steady, contemplative look is essential if we are to penetrate the real meaning of the crucifixion. And the hymn helps us to do this. When Watts first published it the hymn began:

> When I survey the wondrous cross,
> Where the young Prince of glory died.

Two years later, in response to certain criticism, he altered the second line to its present form; but many will agree that the change was regrettable and unnecessary. It is surely worth remembering that when Jesus died on the cross he was still in his early thirties. He laid down his life in the full vigour of his manhood. And this is a point we do well to bear in mind when faced with the seeming tragedy of a human life cut short in the service of God. Inevitably we ask, Why should it happen? But it happened to the young Prince of glory. The value of life is measured not in length of years but in terms of achievement.

As we now turn to the hymn we may learn at least three things about the cross: what it forbids, what it reveals, and what it demands.

1 What the cross forbids

The second stanza teaches us this:

> Forbid it, Lord, that I should boast,
> Save in the death of Christ my God;
> All the vain things that charm me most,
> I sacrifice them to his blood.

The cross at once puts an end to all our boasting. It robs us of every bit of self-esteem and self-satisfaction. When by faith we look at the crucified Son of God and recognize that he died for our sins, we reassess our scale of values:

> My richest gain I count but loss,
> And pour contempt on all my pride.

Here Watts is thinking of St Paul's words to the Philippians: 'What things were gain to me, those I counted loss for Christ' (3.7). The apostle was recalling his past attempts, as a self-righteous Pharisee, to make himself acceptable to God by his religious works and merits. In the light of the cross he saw it all as sheet loss. His own righteousness was simply not good enough for God. Instead, he had to humble himself and pour contempt on all his pride. As a Christian he no longer boasted about what *he* had done but only of what Christ had done for him. 'God forbid that I should glory, save in the cross of our Lord Jesus Christ.' That is now his confession and it must be ours too. The cross is the one thing we may boast about, the thing of supreme worth: God's saving act accomplished once and for all in the death of Christ. All other boasting is forbidden.

We *glory* in the cross! Perhaps we hardly realize what a contradictory statement that appears to be. In the ancient Roman world crucifixion was not only the most terrible but also the most shameful form of death. The victim who hung on a cross was disgraced and discredited in the eyes of men. The cross was the symbol of utmost shame. Yet here Paul is saying, 'I glory in the cross of Jesus Christ. I am not ashamed of my crucified Lord. The shame is mine, not his. I have nothing of my own to be proud of. My only boast is this, that Christ died for me.'

2 What the cross reveals

We take another look at the cross, and what do we see?

Something very wonderful:

> See from his head, his hands, his feet,
> > Sorrow and love flow mingled down;
> Did e'er such love and sorrow meet,
> > Or thorns compose so rich a crown?

The imagery here is derived from St John's account of the crucifixion. The evangelist tells us that a soldier, in order to ensure that Jesus was really dead, 'pierced his side with a spear, and at once there came out blood and water'. Isaac Watts, with a touch of poetic imagination, perhaps a flash of spiritual genius, gazes at the scene and sees not blood and water but 'sorrow and love flow mingled down'. What is the significance of that?

In the *sorrow* of the Saviour on the cross we can surely discern his sorrow for *sin*: the sin of the world for which he suffered and died. He was 'a man of sorrows and acquainted with grief' because 'he was wounded for our transgressions', as the prophet had foretold (Isaiah 53.3,5). So likewise we see in the *love* of the Saviour on the cross his love for the *sinner*; for 'while we were yet sinners Christ died for us' (Romans 5.8). True, it was our sin which took Jesus to the cross, but it was his love for us that held him there, not the nails of the Roman soldiers.

The poet asks, 'Did e'er such love and sorrow meet?' No, never! And again, Did ever 'thorns compose so rich a crown?' It is an astonishing suggestion! To the believer, gazing with reverent adoration on the crucified Saviour, the cruel wreath of thorns encircling his brow is transfigured into a glittering diadem, a monarch's crown. The man of sorrows is the king of love.

3 What the cross demands

In face of such a revelation we cannot remain indifferent or impassive. The cross confronts us with the claims of redeeming love and demands a response which is both personal and complete:

> Were the whole realm of nature mine,
> That were a present far too small;
> Love so amazing, so divine,
> Demands my soul, my life, my all.

In the cross we see the measure of our indebtedness to Christ. He gave everything for us. What are we to give to him? 'The whole realm of nature' to which the hymn refers is not ours to give. In any case such an impersonal offering would be an inadequate return for all that Christ has done for us, 'a present far too small'.

There is only one thing we can give and that is *ourselves*, the whole of ourselves: 'my soul, my life, my all'. My *soul* is what I am as an individual, my essential personality. My *life* is what I do, my daily work and activities. My *all* is what I have, my gifts and talents, my wealth and posessions.

This is what the cross demands. And let us be clear that the demand remains, whether we respond to it or not. Nothing can alter the fact that Christ died for us or diminish the claims his love makes upon us. The verdict rests with us. When in his later years William Booth was asked why it was that God had used him so greatly in his service, he answered, 'I don't know, unless it is that when I gave myself to the Lord I gave all that there was of me.' Total love demands total surrender.

42

11.

WHY DID JESUS DIE?

There is a green hill far away
(Mrs C. F. Alexander, 1818–95)

This hymn was written by a young Irishwoman, Fanny Humphreys. It comes from her *Hymns for Little Children*, dedicated to her young godsons and published in 1848. Two years later she married William Alexander, later to become Bishop of Derry and finally Archbishop of Armagh. So it is that her name is now known to us as Mrs Cecil Frances Alexander.

Her little book met with enormous success. The hymns were designed to illustrate the Church Catechism, so as to make it more attractive and intelligible to young children. The three which have survived, and which are to be found in every hymn book, come from the section dealing with the Creed. Thus, to illustrate the words 'Maker of heaven and earth' is the hymn, 'All things bright and beautiful'; for 'born of the Virgin Mary' is 'Once in royal David's city'; and for 'suffered under Pontius Pilate' is the hymn we are now thinking about, 'There is a green hill far away'.

The purpose of this hymn is to answer the question, Why did Jesus die? And because it is written for children it begins not by preaching a sermon but by painting a picture – the picture of 'a green hill far away'. Ireland abounds in green hills and Fanny Humphreys must have been familiar with many of them. Perhaps it was the view of some grassy slope outside the city walls of Derry that inspired her to write:

> There is a green hill far away,
>   Without a city wall,
> Where the dear Lord was crucified,
>   Who died to save us all.

This opening stanza not only sets the scene of the crucifixion. It does more than that. It records both the historical fact that 'the dear Lord was crucified' and the Christian belief that he 'died to save us all'. But how are we to understand that belief? What does the cross really mean? The verses that follow teach us to remember three things.

1 The mystery of the cross

In seeking to understand the meaning of the cross we do well to be cautious and recognize our ignorance. So the second stanza begins with a word of warning:

> We may not know, we cannot tell,
>   What pains he had to bear,
> But we believe it was for us
>   He hung and suffered there.

We may not know, we cannot tell. . . . There are depths of meaning in the death of Jesus that are beyond our grasp. We are in the presence of mystery. None of us can boast that we know all about the atonement. None of us can explain all that Jesus suffered on the cross. We may have some idea of his physical suffering, but what can we know of his spiritual anguish? 'The Lord laid on him the iniquity of us all.' 'He who knew no sin was made sin for us.'

In biblical statements like these we may discern the clue to our Lord's passion. He bore *our* sins. That at least is clear. We may not and cannot understand the whole of the mystery, but we can affirm with the utmost confidence that 'it was *for us* he died and suffered there'. While the cross happened, so to speak, outside of us, apart from us, we are directly involved in it, because it was for our sake and for our sin that Jesus died.

2 The purpose of the cross

The third stanza – the heart of the whole hymn – spells out in more precise terms the purpose of the Lord's death.

> He died that we might be forgiven,
> He died to make us good,
> That we might go at last to heaven,
> Saved by his precious blood.

Three bold statements are made here. They refer in turn to the past, the present, and the future.

Why did Jesus die? First, *that we might be forgiven.* That is our fundamental need, for it is concerned with our guilty past. The cross goes to the root of the human predicament by restoring the broken relationship with God caused by man's sin. And the result is – reconciliation. What a glorious word! Sin has been dealt with, and dealt with by God, who in Christ was reconciling the world to himself. The enmity is over. We are forgiven. We have peace with God.

But more. Jesus not only died that we might be forgiven. *He died to make us good.* This is what in theological language we call sanctification. Mrs Alexander puts it in simpler terms because she is writing for children, not for theologians. Our being made good – our becoming holy or Christ-like – is a present experience and a lifelong process. It is not a human achievement. It happens as the Holy Spirit works *in* us what Christ wrought *for* us on the cross. But it does demand our co-operation. God cannot 'make us good' unless we allow him to do so and open our lives to him and partake of the means of grace.

Forgiveness for the past, holiness in our present life – but that is not all. For Jesus died *that we might go at last to heaven.* This is the future tense of salvation. The next stanza has something further to say on the matter, for it tells how Jesus, by his one perfect sacrifice for sin, unlocked the gate of heaven, that at last we might pass through that gate into the glory of God's presence.

What a challenge there is for us here!

> O, dearly, dearly has he loved,
>   And we must love him too,
> And trust in his redeeming blood,
>   And try his works to do.

The challenge is threefold. The love of Christ revealed in the cross first claims our *love* in grateful response. 'We love him because he first loved us.' Linked with this is the response of *faith*, our firm trust in the Saviour's redeeming blood. And finally *obedience* – 'And try his works to do'. For faith without works is dead. The two belong together and can never be separated.

We who confess the faith of Christ crucified reveal that faith, not simply by what we say but by what we do. If it is all saying and not doing, our faith is worthless. Jesus warned us about that. 'Not everyone who calls me "Lord, Lord" will enter the kingdom of heaven, but only those who do the will of my heavenly Father.'

12.

KING OF GLORY

At the name of Jesus
(Caroline M. Noel, 1817–77)

This is not the sort of hymn you would have expected to be written by a frail Victorian lady who was, on her own admission, 'incapacitated by weakness'. It seems to have too much vigour and vitality about it for that. But the author, Caroline Maria Noel, though weak in body, was strong in faith, and her hymn reflects that fact.

She composed it as a processional hymn for Ascensiontide. It is based on the well known passage in the Epistle to the Philippians (2.6–11) which itself is almost certainly an early Christian hymn on the humiliation and exaltation of Christ. The apostle quotes it to illustrate his plea for a humble and selfless spirit on the part of his readers. He points them to the supreme example of Christ, who, though originally sharing the essential nature of God, in his incarnate life made himself nothing, took our human flesh and suffered the shameful death of the cross.

That, strictly speaking, is the end of the apostle's illustration. But he cannot leave Jesus there on the cross. That is not the end of the story; so he continues his quotation:

> Therefore God highly exalted him,
>   and gave him the name which is above every
>   name,
> that at the name of Jesus every knee should bow,
>   in heaven, on earth, and under the earth,
> and every tongue confess that Jesus Christ is Lord,
>   to the glory of God the Father.

1 Jesus is Lord

Miss Noel begins her hymn with words borrowed from this triumphant climax;

> At the name of Jesus
>   Every knee shall bow,
> Every tongue confess him
>   King of glory now;

47

'Tis the Father's pleasure
We should call him Lord,
Who from the beginning
Was the mighty Word.

To save misunderstanding, let us be clear that the hymn is not about the name 'Jesus', or bowing at the name. It is about acknowledging the majesty and glory inherent in his divine person. Symbolically we bow the knee to him because, as the hymn says, 'it is the Father's pleasure we should call him Lord'. Yes, *Lord* ! That is the name above every name which God has bestowed on the exalted Christ. It is the name (*kyrios*) used in the Greek version of the Old Testament to render the ineffable name of God himself, *Jahweh*, or Jehovah. Therefore to call Jesus 'Lord' is to recognize not only his sovereignty but also his deity. Before the earth was made or time existed, he was 'the mighty Word'.

This calls to mind the prologue to St John's Gospel: 'When all things began, the Word already was . . . and what God was, the Word was'. Jesus is God manifest in the flesh. Moreover, 'through him all things came into being; no single thing was created without him'. This truth of Christ as the agent of creation was clearly in Miss Noel's mind when she wrote the second stanza, beginning:

At his voice creation
Sprang at once to sight;

and creation here includes the spiritual realm as well as the physical, things heavenly as well as earthly.

2 Jesus the Saviour

The next stanza reverts to the opening part of the early Christian hymn which St Paul quotes, the part dealing with our Lord's self-humiliation. The eternal Son 'emptied himself' of his heavenly glory – but not, let us be clear, of his divine nature – and became man for man's salvation.

> Humbled for a season,
>   To receive a name
> From the lips of sinners
>   Unto whom he came;
> Faithfully he bore it,
>   Spotless to the last,
> Brought it back victorious
>   When from death he passed.

'Humbled for a season.' Those four words at the beginning of the verse cover the whole of Jesus' life and ministry. He took the lowly form of a servant or slave to receive a certain name. What was it? Surely it was the lovely name of 'Saviour', the name bestowed on him by 'sinners'. It was to *them* he came: to those who recognized their need of him and found in him the answer to their need. He came to seek and save the *lost*. His salvation is for sinners only.

It was as the sinners' saviour that Jesus faithfully bore that name and pursued his earthly mission 'to the last' – to his death. And then, the saving work accomplished, he passed victoriously from death to life, the risen Lord.

Next comes the ascension, which is the main theme of this hymn. The fourth stanza continues without a break from the previous one and describes how Jesus bore that saving name to heaven:

> Bore it up triumphant
>   With its human light,
> Through all ranks of creatures,
>   To the central height . . .

The language here is richly poetical, not literal. Do we find it difficult? That is not surprising, for it is dealing with things unseen and eternal, things far beyond our finite minds. But the meaning is unmistakable. It is indicated not so much in the

49

words as in the movement, which is all upward and heaven-
ward, higher and yet higher to the very 'throne of Godhead'.

3 Jesus the exalted King

Jesus is the exalted king. The same Jesus who once humbled
himself to this earth, to share our humanity and suffer a
shameful death, now reigns in the highest heaven, crowned
with glory and honour.

What then? Is there anything more to be said? Yes, for up to
this point the hymn has been wholly *objective*. All attention
has been fixed on Christ, and Christ alone. We ourselves have
not come into the picture. But now that changes. We become
directly involved and challenged:

> Name him, brothers, name him,
>   With love as strong as death,
> But with awe and wonder,
>   And with bated breath;
> He is God the Saviour,
>   He is Christ the Lord,
> Ever to be worshipped,
>   Trusted, and adored.

This fifth stanza is not, of course, the final one; but it makes
an admirable finish to the hymn and will well serve that
purpose now. It calls upon us to 'name' Jesus. What does that
signify? Surely to name him in this context is to confess him,
acknowledge his claims, render him homage. We do so with
love, the love of our hearts, 'love as strong as death'. But we do
so also with reverence and a sense of wonder, for he is both
'God the *Saviour*' and 'Christ the *Lord*'.

Those are the two titles specially ascribed to Jesus in this
hymn: Saviour, the name he received from the lips of sinners
on earth, and Lord, the name above every name given him by
the Father in heaven. And this Saviour and Lord is 'ever to be

50

worshipped, trusted and adored'. By whom? By all who yield him their allegiance – and therefore by us as well. In singing this fine hymn we must not be so carried away by the words and music that we fail to bring to the Lord *our* adoration, worship and praise.

13.

CORONATION

The head that once was crowned with thorns
(T. Kelly, 1769–1855)

Thomas Kelly, the author of this hymn, was an Irishman. As the son of a judge he studied for the Bar; but when still a young man he experienced a deep evangelical conversion and dedicated his life to Christ's service. Though originally ordained in the Church of Ireland, he turned Dissenter so as to have greater freedom for preaching the gospel. Being a man of ample means he built chapels in various parts of the country; but he also used his money freely to help the poverty-stricken people of Ireland, especially during the terrible famine of 1847.

He wrote a large number of hymns, among them 'We sing the praise of him who died' and 'The Lord is risen indeed'; but none is finer than 'The head that once was crowned with thorns', a splended hymn for Ascensiontide. It might be called the hymn of Christ's two coronations, the one on earth, the other in heaven. Before his crucifixion the Roman soldiers placed a crown of thorns on his head and offered him mock homage, crying, 'Hail, King of the Jews!' Years later the apostle John in his lonely exile on Patmos was given a vision of

Christ in his celestial glory and saw that 'on his head were many crowns' (Rev.19,12). So we sing:

> The head that once was crowned with thorns
>> Is crowned with glory now;
> A royal diadem adorns
>> The mighty victor's brow.

The hymn falls naturally into two parts. In the first three stanzas our attention is focused on the person of Christ – once crucified, now exalted to the throne. The second part, the last three stanzas, sees in this the pattern of Christian discipleship. As Christ is one with his people, so are they one with him, both in suffering and glory.

1 Christ crucified and glorified

In writing the opening stanza Thomas Kelly had in mind some words in the letter to the Hebrews: 'We see Jesus, who for a short while was made lower than the angels, crowned with glory and honour because of the suffering of death' (2.9). In that single sentence the incarnation, the passion, and the exaltation of Christ are brought together. It is a miniature creed, with the cross at the centre. We must not fail to take note of that, for the cross is central to our faith. But we not only see Jesus crucified. We also see him crowned: 'a royal diadem adorns the mighty victor's brow'. When the Lord had completed his earthly mission he returned to heaven as conqueror. He had fully and finally accomplished the work he had come to do; and so, in the language of the Bible and the creed, he 'sat down at the right hand of God'. The hymn explains what that means:

> The highest place that heaven affords
>> Is his, is his by right,
> The King of kings and Lord of lords,
>> And heaven's eternal light.

The picture is that of Christ in majesty. The Lamb is on the throne. Jesus is King. Nothing so sustains our faith in dark and difficult times as the assurance that our Lord reigns and that all authority is his in heaven and on earth. And that is why, as the hymn does on to say (v.3), he is the *joy* of his people, whether they dwell above or below. Heaven rings with the praises of the redeemed: 'To him who sits on the throne, and to the lamb, be praise and honour, glory and might, for every and ever!' (Rev.5.13). The Church on earth echoes their song.

2 *The cross and the crown*

We turn now to the second part of the hymn. The picture of Christ crucified and glorified in the first part is not set before us to arouse our wonder or even to evoke our worship. It has something important to teach us. It portrays a pattern of discipleship which directly applies to all who profess to know and follow Christ:

> To them the cross, with all its shame,
>   With all its grace is given:
> Their name an everlasting name,
>   Their joy the joy of heaven.

The cross which Jesus endured for man's salvation is of course unique. His followers have no direct part in that, for it can never be repeated. But they *are* called upon to bear the reproach of the cross and to be prepared to suffer – and suffer joyfully – for their Lord. The old adage, 'No cross, no crown', remains true, as the next stanza says:

> They suffer for their Lord below,
>   They reign with him above,
> Their profit and their joy to know
>   The mystery of his love.

The first two lines echo some words from the second letter to

Timothy, probably part of an early hymn about the believer's identification with Christ:

> If we died with him, we shall also live with him;
> If we endure patiently, we shall also reign with him.

Scholars believe that the words come from a humn about baptism, in which the believer is united with Christ in his death and resurrection. If that is so, the hymn's purpose was to encourage the newly baptized to endure hardship and persecution bravely for Christ's sake, knowing that to suffer with him now is to be glorified with him hereafter (Rom.8.17).

Significantly the cross is the theme of the final stanza:

> The cross he bore is life and health,
>   Though shame and death to him;
> His people's hope, his people's wealth,
>   Their everlasting theme.

What to Jesus was 'shame and death' is 'life and health' to those who confess the faith of Christ crucified. For the cross is his people's *hope*: their one assured hope of salvation in this life and in that which is to come.

The cross is also his people's *wealth*; for in the redemptive work of Christ there are riches of infinite worth, transcending man's understanding and far excelling all earthly treasure.

And the cross is his people's *everlasting theme*, the unchanging theme of their worship on earth and in heaven, for time and for all eternity.

'Worthy is the Lamb, who was slain, to receive all power and wealth, wisdom and might, honour and glory and praise!' (Rev.5.12).

14.

CITY OF GOD

Glorious things of thee are spoken
(J. Newton, 1725–1807)

People often complain and grumble about the Church – their local church or the Church at large – and are only too ready to paint it in the worst possible colours. Here by contrast we have a fine biblical hymn about the Church which glows with confidence and rings with joy.

It was written by that remarkable evangelical clergyman John Newton, one time infidel and captain of a slave ship – 'a full-blooded sinner converted into a full-blooded saint,' as Erik Routley described him. He was also the author of 'How sweet the name of Jesus sounds' and many other hymns, written while he was in charge of the parish of Olney in Buckingham-shire. They were published, along with contributions by the poet William Cowper, in the *Olney Hymns*, 1779.

His hymn about the Church is notable for the numerous symbols and images it employs, all derived from the scriptures and all adding something of value to the total picture of what the Church is in God's design.

1 The City of God

The title Newton gave to the hymn was 'The City of God' and this is the symbol used in the opening stanza.

> Glorious things of thee are spoken,
>   Zion, city of our God;
> He whose word cannot be broken
>   Formed thee for his own abode.

Newton here is drawing on the words of Psalm 87.2,3: 'The Lord loves the gates of Zion more than all the dwelling-places of Jacob. Glorious things are spoken of you, O city of God.' Zion is the poetical name for Jerusalem: the city above all which he had sanctified with his presence. It is therefore a fitting picture of the Church, the true Zion, his dwelling-place by the Spirit. And the city is impregnable:

> On the Rock of Ages founded,
>   What can shake thy sure repose?
> With salvation's walls surrounded,
>   Thou mayest smile at all thy foes.

There is no doubt as to the Rock of Ages on which the Church is founded. 'No other foundation can be laid than that which is laid, which is Jesus Christ' (1 Cor.3.11). He himself said to Simon Peter who had confessed him to be the Messiah, the Son of God, 'On this rock I will build my church, and the powers of death shall not prevail against it'(Matt.16.18). None of the forces of evil at work in the world can vanquish the City of God. Its foundation is strong and immovable. And despite all that its foes may threaten or do, the inhabitants of Zion can joyfully sing, 'We have a strong city whose walls are salvation' (Isa.26.1).

2 The river of life

A city, if it is to flourish, must have water. That is as true today as it was in ancient times. And that of course is why all the great cities of the world are built on the banks of a river.

The hymn applies this to the City of God:

> See, the streams of living waters,
>   Springing from eternal love,
> Well supply thy sons and daughters,
>   And all fear of want remove.

The citizens of Zion – 'thy sons and daughters' – are well cared for by the river which supplies them with 'streams of living water', a river which springs from God's eternal love. Here Newton had in mind the words of another psalm: 'There is a river whose streams make glad the city of God' (Ps.46.4). He may also have recalled the story of the smitten rock from which the water flowed in the wilderness (Ex.17). St Paul, in interpreting the story, gave it a spiritual meaning: 'that rock was Christ' (1 Cor.10.4). From him flows 'living water', as he himself promised (John 7.37), a veritable river of life, abundant, inexhaustible, satisfying.

> Who can faint while such a river
> Ever flows their thirst to assuage?
> Grace, which like the Lord the giver,
> Never fails from age to age.

3 The pillar of fire

Many hymnals omit Newton's third verse, beginning:

> Round each habitation hovering,
> See the cloud and fire appear,
> For a glory and a covering,
> Showing that the Lord is near.

Again the writer refers to the story of the Exodus. In their long journey to the promised land the Israelites were not left to their own devices. God showed them the way. 'The Lord went before them by day in a pillar of cloud to lead them along the way, and by night in a pillar of fire to give them light' (Ex.13.21). This striking piece of symbolism, skilfully woven into the hymn, depicts another aspect of the Church. Now it is not a city but a company of pilgrims on the march. The Lord is with them, their leader and guide by day and night; and, as the second part of the stanza says, he provides them with food for their journey – with manna, the bread from heaven (John 6.32.33).

4 *The citizens of Zion*

The final verse is about membership of the Church. And this is where *we* become involved. In the previous stanzas we have been looking at the Church, so to speak, from the outside; but in very truth each one of us is an insider, not an outsider. So we sing:

> Saviour, since of Zion's city
> I, through grace, a member am,
> Let the world deride or pity,
> I will glory in thy name.

And well may we glory! We are citizens of Zion. We are members of the Church, the society of God's redeemed people, the community of his saints, the body of Christ on earth. To belong to it is the greatest privilege we can enjoy in our present life. Compared with this, what has the world to offer?

> Fading is the worldling's pleasure,
> All his boasted pomp and show;
> Solid joys and lasting treasure
> None but Zion's children know.

Commenting on these words in his essay on this hymn Dr Erik Routley said: 'While the man of the world builds bigger and bigger storehouses for his accumulating property, while he pursues a happiness which is always round the next corner, the Christian will show him how to live, for he knows what sort of pleasure is really solid and lasting, and how to find it.' This is the challenge that church-membership presents to us. And this is what the world has the right to expect from the people of Christ.

58

15.

CHURCH MILITANT

Onward, Christian soldiers
(S. Baring-Gould, 1834–1924)

For the story of this hymn we must travel back in time to the year 1864 and transport ourselves in imagination to the Yorkshire village of Horbury Bridge, near Wakefield. A new curate, Sabine Baring-Gould, had arrived in the parish and taken charge of the mission church. As was then customary in many north country places, on the Whit-Monday there was to be a procession of the Sunday school children to an adjoining village.

Among the hymns to be sung in the procession the curate noted one with a good marching tune by Haydn, but he didn't care much for the words; so he set about writing new words to fit the tune – and the result was 'Onward, Christian soldiers'. The hymn was published in the *Church Times* later in the year and soon became popular. Its popularity was increased when Sir Arthur Sullivan wrote for it the famous tune *St Gertrude* to which it is still sung.

The hymn is sometimes criticized these days because of its outdated language and military imagery. But behind the metaphors there are aspects of Christian truth which are timeless and which we need constantly to think about. Of course the teaching does not go deep, for the hymn was written for children, its purpose being to fire their imagination with a sense of the greatness and glory of Christ's service. But adults delight to sing it as well as children.

The theme of the hymn is the Church militant here on earth. As we look at it let us concentrate our attention on that and not be too critical of the archaic language. What sort of Church is here depicted?

1 The Church on the march

First of all we see a Church on the march:

> Onward, Christian soldiers,
> Marching as to war,
> With the cross of Jesus
> Going on before.

Onward ! The very first word is arresting. The Church is moving. It is not at a standstill or settling down to a comfortable existence. Nor is it bogged down by the past and for ever looking back to the good old days. Its gaze is directed to the future as it moves forward to fresh tasks and further conquests. That is certainly how it should be with the Church of Christ.

Moreover, the Church must move forward with a sense of purpose. It is going somewhere. It is moving in a certain direction as 'Christ the royal Master' leads the way. The church procession, with the cross and banners going on ahead, gives pictorial expression to this idea. But let us be clear: Christ leads his people *out* of the Church *into* the world; for his last command to his disciples was to carry the good news of God's redeeming love to all nations. That command represents the Church's marching orders in every generation and the challenge confronts us still.

2 The Church in conflict

Not only is the Church marching. It is 'marching as to war'. There is a conflict to be fought, a foe to be faced and conquered.

60

> At the sign of triumph
>   Satan's legions flee;
> On then, Christian soldiers,
>   On to victory.

The Christian warfare is not a phoney one. It is essentially of a spiritual character but it is none the less real on that account. In urging Christ's soldiers to put on the whole armour of God, St Paul says: 'Our fight is not against human foes but against cosmic powers, against the spiritual forces of evil in the heavenly realms' (Eph.6.12).

Beyond question there is an active power of evil at work in the world, what the hymn calls 'Satan's legions'. Evil takes many shapes and forms: political, social, intellectual – yes, and religious, for Satan is expert at disguising himself as an angel of light (2 Cor.11.14). This is why the Church must be ready for battle. It cannot remain neutral, or compromise with evil, or adopt a pacifist role. Rather it must carry the war into the enemy's camp as it strives for the furtherance of God's kingdom in an increasingly secular and pagan society.

3 The Church – Christ's army

In fighting this battle we are not left to struggle on our own. As soldiers of Christ we are part of a great army, and that is a big consolation. A soldier is nothing apart from the army, apart from his comrades; as the hymn reminds us:

> Like a mighty army
>   Moves the Church of God;
> Brothers, we are treading
>   Where the saints have trod.

The 'mighty army' here referred to is not the local congregation, which may be no more than a handful of godly, faithful souls. Yet, few though they may be, they are part of a great and glorious company, the fellowship of the saints, nothing less than Christ's one, holy, catholic and apostolic Church. There is enormous strength in the recollection of that truth. The individual soldier may not count for much. He cannot by himself win any war. But going into battle as part of the army he can rightfully claim his share in the army's victory. So it is with those who serve under Christ's banner. And ultimate victory is assured, for Christ's army, the Church, is invincible, as the fourth stanza boldy affirms.

4 The Church enlisting recruits

The hymn's final stanza calls upon others to enlist for Christ:

> Onward, then, ye people,
> Join our happy throng,
> Blend with ours your voices
> In the triumph song.

An army constantly needs recruits if it is to maintain its strength. In times of emergency a special recruiting campaign may be necessary. The Christian army is perpetually engaged in such a campaign. We call it evangelism. 'Join our happy throng' is the Church's invitation to all who have not yet given their personal allegiance to Jesus Christ as Saviour and Lord. It is an invitation to everyone who wants to find a worthwhile purpose in life and serve the greatest of all causes, the kingdom of God.

What about ourselves here? Have we enlisted for Christ? Remember, he wants no conscripts in his army. he wants only willing recruits. Perhaps there is such a recruit in this church today.

16.

UNSLEEPING CHURCH

The day thou gavest, Lord, is ended
(J. Ellerton, 1826–93)

We inevitably regard this as an evening hymn and in one sense
of course it is. In the hymn books it is always classified as such,
for its opening stanza renders it suitable for use only at the
evening hour:

> The day thou gavest, Lord, is ended,
> The darkness falls at thy behest;
> To thee our morning hymns ascended,
> Thy praise shall sanctify our rest.

But in fact the work was not written primarily as an evening
hymn. When first published in 1870 it formed part of an order
of service for missionary meetings and its missionary character
is undeniable. Its author was Canon John Ellerton, a leading
hymnologist of his day.

Of the many hymns he wrote this is certainly the finest:
beautifully phrased, perfectly shaped, and vividly pictorial. It is
the sort of hymn that not only captures the imagination but
kindles faith. And it is well matched by the tune *St Clement*
composed for it by a young clergyman, Clement Schoefield.
Note his Christian name, for it was that which suggested to
Arthur Sullivan (later Sir Arthur) the title of the tune when it
was first published in a hymnal he edited.

The hymn portrays various aspects of the Church's life and
work.

1 A missionary body

First of all it bears witness to the Church's fulfilment of its
missionary task, its obedience to the commission of the risen
Lord: 'Go forth and make disciples from among all nations'
(Matt.28.19). In saying that, the Lord constituted his Church
as a missionary body – that is, a body of people committed to
mission. He entrusted to his disciples the responsibility of
making more disciples, far and wide. The whole Church was
intended to be a society for the propagation of the gospel.

The hymn does not directly refer to the Lord's commission
or to the Church's obedience to it, but both are implicit in the
hymn as a whole. The very fact that we here today can sing of
the Church in other lands testifies to the success attending the
Christian mission. So it is that, in one place or another,

> The voice of prayer is never silent,
> Nor dies the strain of praise away.

The churches in those distant places are the fruit of long and
patient missionary endeavour. Thus indirectly the hymn wit-
nesses to what has been accomplished by the Church in the
past. At the same time it encourages the Church in the present
to maintain and extend its work overseas. The Church must
constantly see itself as a missionary body, with the whole world
as its parish and all mankind as its potential membership.

2 A worldwide fellowship

Arising out of this is the concept of the Church as a worldwide
fellowship. This is the dominant note in the hymn. It begins
with the imagery of morning and evening, day and night; but
this is no more than a pictorial background, to illustrate the
truth that while one part of the earth sleeps, another part is
waking and praising God.

We thank thee that thy Church unsleeping,
    While earth rolls onward into light,
Through all the world her watch is keeping,
    And rests not now by day and night.

And again:

The sun that bids us rest is waking
    Our brethren 'neath the western sky.

The picture of the unsleeping Church is very striking. While night falls in one land, day is breaking in another and there is never a time when in some part of the globe the Church is not watching and working and praising God. The hymn thus creates in the singer a sense of the Church's universality. Indeed, it almost gives the impression that all nations have heard the gospel and that the Church has taken root in every country.

That certainly was not the case when the hymn was written well over a hundred years ago. The modern missionary movement was then still in its infancy. Vast areas of the world remained unevangelized. However, the latter part of the nineteenth century was marked by rapid missionary expansion, and in some measure this was commensurate with the growth of the British Empire.

It is not without significance, therefore, that when in 1897 Queen Victoria celebrated her Diamond Jubilee she chose this hymn to be sung at the thanksgiving services held in thousands of churches and chapels. The hymn's immense popularity dates from this time. The Queen may well have regarded her vast domains – 'the empire on which the sun never sets' – as a symbol of the worldwide Church.

But the Church must never be thought of imperially, in terms of a territorial empire. The hymn's final stanza warns us that 'earth's proud empires pass away'. God's kingdom, of which the Church is the representative and agent, is something very different, as Jesus plainly taught us. That kingdom is spiritual, not geographical. It recognizes no racial or national boundaries. Likewise the Church of Christ is a fellowship of the Spirit and its door is wide open to people of every nation upon earth.

3 A worshipping community

The hymn depicts a third aspect of the Church. This universal fellowship, in whatever part of the earth it is found, is represented as a worshipping community.

The note is struck in the opening verse, which refers to our morning hymns and our evening praise. And the worship *we* thus offer in our own land is continued by the unsleeping Church in other parts of the world. The voice of prayer, the strain of praise, is unceasingly prolonged, for as 'the earth rolls onward into light' it comes about that

> . . . hour by hour fresh lips are making
> Thy wondrous doings heard on high.

The 'fresh lips' are those of our Christian brothers and sisters awaking on the other side of the globe while we lie down to sleep. They are awaking to proclaim God's 'wondrous doings' in songs of praise.

This portrayal of the Church as a worshipping community is clear enough. It is a picture to keep constantly before us, for worship is fundamental to the Christian life. It glorifies the Lord. It lifts us out of ourselves. It prepares us for the life of the world to come, where all is praise. And it fortifies our faith in the sovereignty of God:

> So be it; Lord; thy throne shall never,
>   Like earth's proud empires, pass away;
> Thy kingdom stands, and grows for ever,
>   Till all thy creatures own thy sway.

17.

THE ONE OBLATION

And now, O Father, mindful of the love
(W. Bright, 1824–1901)

Canon Scott Holland of St Paul's Cathedral said of this hymn: 'As long as our Church lives, we shall sing at the most sacred hours "And now, O Father, mindful of the love". It is worth living for to have left behind one such hymn which will be sung by unnumbered generations.' Its author was Canon William Bright, who also wrote another well-known communion hymn, 'Once, only once, and once for all. He was a distinguished scholar and for many years served as Professor of Ecclesiastical History of Oxford.

People may sometimes wonder why this hymn begins with the conjuction 'And'. Several other hymns do the same, often for no apparent reason. But in this case there is a simple explanation. The four stanzas we sing are not the complete hymn as it was written but the latter part only. The previous verses provided the background to the Communion service. With the 'And now' the service proper begins, with our active participation in the sacrament; and as we shall see, each of the stanzas touches on a particular aspect of the sacrament.

1 Remembrance

Remembrance is the keynote of the first stanza. We call to mind the redeeming love of God in the sacrifice of his Son:

> And now, O Father, mindful of the love
> That bought us, once for all, on Calvary's tree,

67

And having with us him that pleads above,
　　We here present, we here spread forth to thee
　That only offering perfect in thine eyes,
　　The one true, pure, immortal sacrifice.

The Communion service finds its centre in the cross. It is a continual memorial of Christ's passion. At the passover meal, when Jesus gave his disciples the broken bread and outpoured wine, he said 'Do this in remembrance of me'.

The Greek word for remembrance (*anamnesis*) means the recalling of past events in such a way as to make them a present reality. The Jews at their passover vividly recalled and relived the nation's mighty deliverance from the bondage of Egypt. At the Eucharist Christians celebrate a yet greater redemption. As Christ's saving work on the cross is made present and real to us, we become in some way involved in his sacrifice. We do not and cannot repeat that sacrifice, for it is unique. It has been done, as the hymn says, 'once for all, on Calvary's tree'. It is 'the one true, pure, immortal sacrifice'. But we 'present' it or show it forth in sacramental form; for as the apostle said, as often as we partake of the bread and wine we 'proclaim the Lord's death until he comes'.

2 Penitence

The second stanza takes on a penitential character as we relate Christ's saving work to ourselves and acknowledge our unworthiness.

　　Look, Father, look on his anointed face,
　　　And only look on us as found in him;
　　Look not on our misusings of thy grace,
　　　Our prayer so languid, and our faith so dim.

These words have been likened to the prayer of humble access in the Communion service. We do not presume to come

68

to the Lord's table trusting in our own righteousness but in God's manifold and great mercies. 'We are not worthy,' we confess, 'so much as to gather up the crumbs under thy table.' So now in the hymn we ask the Father to look on the face of his anointed Son, the Christ of Calvary, and only to 'look on us as found in him'. To be 'found in Christ' was St Paul's ambition, as he told the Philippians, for he had no righteousness of his own – only 'that which is through faith in Christ' (Phil.3.9).

We go on to confess the lament our misusings of God's grace, and this includes our neglect of it: 'our prayer so languid, and our faith so dim'. Surely we all know something of that! We are indeed 'miserable sinners' – that is, as the term means, sinners in need of God's mercy; and it is to his mercy and not to our merits that we trust:

> For lo, between our sins and their reward
> We set the passion of thy Son our Lord.

3 Intercession

Another aspect of the Communion is now introduced: intercession, or prayer for others. In the forms of intercession in our prayer books we pray in general terms for 'the whole Church of God in Christ Jesus, and for all men according to their needs'. It is right that we should do so, for at the last supper our Lord prayed not only for his disciples but for the Church of the future (John 17). We must not be so wrapped up in our worship that we forget the greater Church throughout the world.

In the hymn we intercede particularly for our loved ones:

> And then for those, our dearest and our best,
> By this prevailing presence we appeal. . .

And what do we ask that God will grant them? Not merely the things connected with their temporal well-being but the things of highest worth: 'O do thine utmost for their souls' true weal', that is, for their spiritual welfare. In the end this is what matters most. We can ask for them nothing better than what the hymn suggests: that they may be guarded from the evil of the world, be preserved in purity of soul and body, and be given God's crowning gift of perseverance in following Christ.

4 Petition

Having prayed for others we finally pray for ourselves. That would seem to be the right order: first intercession, then petition.

> And so we come; O draw us to thy feet,
>   Most patient Saviour who canst love us still;
> And by this food, so awful and so sweet,
>   Deliver us from every touch of ill:
> In thine own service make us glad and free,
> And grant us never more to part with thee.

'And so we come' – not simply to the Lord's table but to the Lord himself. In the previous verses we have been addressing God the Father. Now we are speaking to the Lord Jesus, our 'most patient Saviour' who can love us still – and who does love us still, despite our faithlessness and all our failures. That is a marvellously encouraging thought. And because of his un-changing and unending love we ask him to draw us closer to himself, to deliver us from all that is spiritually harmful, to give us both joy and freedom in his service, and to keep us in unbroken communion with him till the end of our days.

These are big things to ask, and things worth asking for. Let us think about them as we sing them, so that we may sing with the understanding, and mean what we pray.

18.

COMMUNION

Here, O my Lord, I see thee face to face
(H. Bonar, 1808–89)

This beautiful Communion hymn by Dr Horatius Bonar, the distinguished Scottish minister and hymn-writer [see no. 32] recalls the story of an old Scotswoman many years ago. When she became too infirm to attend the quarterly Communion service at the kirk she would wait patiently at home to welcome the family on their return. She would then talk to the young people and inquire, 'Did you meet anyone in the service?' They would mention the name of various neighbours and friends, whereupon she gently insisted, 'Yes, I know about those, but did you meet anyone special in the service?' Her meaning was now clear. To that godly old woman the Lord's supper was a meeting with the Lord Jesus himself.

It was this thought, seemingly, that inspired Dr Bonar to write his hymn. In rich devotional language it spells out the meaning of the sacrament for the faithful communicant. Let us look at some of the stanzas (there were originally ten in all) and seek to learn something for ourselves.

1 A trysting place with Christ

First and foremost the sacrament should be a trysting place with Christ.

> Here, O my Lord, I see thee face to face;
>   Here I would touch and handle things unseen;
> Here grasp with firmer hand the eternal grace,
>   And all my weariness upon thee lean.

71

Face to face with Christ! *He* assuredly is the centre of our eucharistic worship. It was he who ordained the sacrament. It was he who presided at the paschal meal in the upper room. It was he who said of the bread and wine, 'This is my body', 'This is my blood'. And it was he who bade us 'Do this in memory of me'. Yes, of *me*: apart from the person of Christ the sacrament is devoid of meaning. 'The cup of blessing which we bless, is it not a participation in the blood of Christ? The bread which we break, is it not a participation in the body of Christ?' (1 Cor. 10.16).

At the Lord's table we do indeed 'touch and handle things unseen'. But most important of all we meet with the unseen Lord and lay hold by faith of the benefits of his passion. Exactly *how* Christ is present in the sacrament has been debated endlessly by Christian scholars. For devout believers the question is a purely academic one. However little they can explain or rationalize it, they know in experience the reality of the Lord's presence. As we have said, he is the giver of the feast and what he gives to his people is the gift of himself in all the virtue of his atoning death, in all the energy of his risen life.

2 A joyous feast

'The Lord's supper' is one of the earliest names given to the sacrament (1 Cor.11.20). A supper is a relaxed and happy evening meal, a time when the members of the family sit down together and enjoy one another's company. Should not the supper of the Lord have something of that character? Bonar thought so:

> This is the hour of banquet and of song,
>> This is the heavenly table spread for me;
> Here let me feast, and feasting still prolong
>> The brief bright hour of fellowship with thee.

In the sacrament of his body and blood the Lord invites us not to a ritual but to a banquet. The 'heavenly table' is spread for us all. It is a time of feasting and fellowship. And it is a time of *song*. The note of praise and thanksgiving should therefore be dominant in the eucharist. We read in the Gospels that, at the end of the last supper, Jesus and his disciples joined in an act of praise. 'When they had sung a hymn, they went out to the mount of Olives.'

A joyous feast! Such it should be. But is not the note of joy too often missing from our Communions? Are we not inclined to approach the service in a strangely sombre spirit? There is of course a proper place for solemnity in the sacrament, for it is a memorial of the Lord's passion. But it is far more than that. It is the celebration of his triumph over sin and death. We come to meet with the risen Saviour and the frame of mind in which we come should be one of exultant joy and overflowing thanksgiving.

3 A means of grace

Praise is what we offer to the Lord in this service. Grace is what he offers to us, for the sacrament is pre-eminently a means of grace.

We come to him in all our need. He is there to meet our need. We come to him with a deep sense of our sins and failures, our unworthiness, our faithlessness. In penitence we kneel at the cross and confess our wrong doing; and there he meets with us and grants us the grace of absolution.

> Mine is the sin, but thine the righteousness;
>   Mine is the guilt, but thine the cleansing blood;
> Here is my robe, my refuge, and my peace,
>   Thy blood, thy righteousness, O Lord my God.

Or again, we come in all our weakness of soul, conscious of our need of strength for life's battle. How can we win the

73

victory? The Lord not only has the answer. He himself *is* the answer. His grace is sufficient. So in faith we sing:

> I have no help but thine; nor do I need
>   Another arm save thine to lean upon;
> It is enough, my Lord, enough indeed;
>   My strength is in thy might, thy might alone.

4 *A foretaste of heaven*

Bonar's final stanza points to another aspect of the sacrament, and one we are inclined to overlook. St Paul, after recording our Lord's words and actions at the institution, wrote: 'As often as you eat this bread and drink the cup, you proclaim the Lord's death until he comes' (1 Cor.11.26). The sacrament thus reminds us that we are living between the two advents of Christ. It looks back to his cross and passion; it looks forward to his final triumph. And *then* the sacrament will be no longer needed. We celebrate it only 'until he comes'.

> Feast after feast thus comes and passes by,
>   Yet passing, points to the glad feast above,
> Giving sweet foretaste of the festal joy,
>   The Lamb's great bridal feast of bliss and love.

There will be no Communion service in heaven, for heaven will be unbroken communion with Christ. The Lord's family will then be at home with him at 'the glad feast above'. Meanwhile, at his table here on earth, his people have a foretaste of what is to come. Memory and hope are blended, and thus the sacrament proclaims the whole gospel in miniature: Christ had died! Christ is risen! Christ will come again!

19.

PRAYER

Lord, teach us how to pray aright
(J. Montgomery, 1771–1854)

This hymn reads rather like the outline of a sermon on prayer, even though it is addressed to God. Its 'text' is the request of the disciples to Jesus, 'Lord, teach us to pray, as John also taught his disciples' (Luke 11.1). Having observed their Master at prayer they recognized how real prayer was to him and how much they had to learn about it. So they asked him to teach them. We too need to learn how to pray aright, for we are all very much beginners in the school of prayer.

The hymn was written by James Montgomery, the foremost English hymn-writer in the first part of the last century. He was a deeply dedicated layman, a Sheffield journalist who used his flare for words in writing devotional verse of a high quality. Here in this hymn, in sermonic manner, he makes a number of valuable 'points' about prayer.

1 Preparing to pray

Montgomery entitled his hymn 'The preparations of the heart in man' and the first two stanzas are concerned largely with these preparations.

> Lord, teach us how to pray aright
>   With reverence and with fear;
> Though dust and ashes in thy sight,
>   We may, we must, draw near.

Reverence, or godly fear, is a basic preparation of the heart

75

for prayer. For when we pray we are entering into communion with the high and holy one, compared with whom we are but 'dust and ashes'. Yet even so 'we may and must draw near' to him. The *may* denotes the privilege of prayer, for the way to the Father is always open. The *must* denotes the necessity of prayer, for spiritually speaking we cannot live without it. As Montgomery says in another hymn, 'Prayer is the Christian's vital breath, the Christian's native air'. So this one continues:

> We perish if we cease from prayer;
> O grant us power to pray;
> And when to meet thee we prepare,
> Lord, meet us by the way.

The power to pray, as well as the desire to pray, is the gift of God. 'We do not know how to pray as we ought,' says the apostle, 'but the Spirit comes to the aid of our weakness' (Rom.8.26). We do well to pause and ask for the Spirit's aid as we prepare to meet with God; and we may be sure that he is always ready, and more than ready, to meet with us.

2 Humility and sincerity

We learn something more about how we are to approach the Father.

> God of all grace, we come to thee
> With broken contrite hearts;
> Give, what thine eye delights to see,
> Truth in the inward parts.

We come to God 'with broken contrite hearts' (see Psalm 51.17). That denotes a humble spirit; and humility is never more essential than when we pray. True humility is a rare thing. It has been defined as 'facing the truth about who God is, and the truth about who I am' (Basil Hume). To recognize the greatness and glory of God is to acknowledge our own littleness and unworthiness.

Our Lord's parable of the Pharisee and the tax collector (Luke 18.9–14) illustrates this. Both men went to the temple to pray, but only one of them actually did so. The Pharisee merely talked to himself – and about himself. He boasted of his own goodness. He believed himself to be superior to others. He suffered from that deadly disease, spiritual pride. The tax collector on the other hand knew the truth about himself. With 'broken contrite heart' he could only keep on saying, 'God, be merciful to me a sinner'. And it was this man who went home 'justified' or acquitted, not the other.

With humility goes something else that God delights to see, 'truth in the inward parts'. This is sincerity, the opposite of sham. True prayer is the lifting up of the heart and mind to God, not just the lifting up of the hands or voice. It is far more than repeating words. It means being aware of God, desiring him, enjoying intimate fellowship with him. Without that, prayer is only a pretence.

3 Faith and patience

Another requirement is faith:

> Faith in the only sacrifice
> That can for sin atone;
> To cast our hopes, to fix our eyes,
> On Christ, on Christ alone.

In prayer we come to God trusting in the merits and mediation of the Lord Jesus Christ. As the Epistle to the Hebrews puts it, 'We have confidence to enter the most holy place' – that is, God's presence – 'by the blood of Jesus, by the new and living way which he opened for us'; and so comes the invitation, 'Let us draw near to God with a sincere heart in full

77

assurance of faith' (Heb.10.19–22). We come to the Father through the Son. We fix all our hopes 'on Christ, and Christ alone'. It is this that gives confidence to our prayers.

Prayer also calls for patience and perseverance.

> Patience to watch, and wait, and weep,
>   Though mercy long delay;
> Courage our fainting souls to keep,
>   And trust thee though thou slay.

Our prayers are not always answered at once or in the way we desire. We should not be surprised at this, for Jesus taught us to keep on praying and never lose heart (Luke 18.1).

Sometimes our prayers are not answered at all, or so it seems, and we become discouraged. It is then that we need what the hymn calls 'courage our fainting souls to keep' and to trust God still. It is perfectly right to ask God for things; Jesus taught us to do so. But we must never dictate to God. *We* do not know what is best, either for ourselves or for others. *He* may have a better and wiser plan. Even so, let us be sure that asking is not in vain or a waste of time, for the very act of asking draws us closer to God; and this is what matters in the end.

'Lord, teach us how to pray aright': that was the beginning of the hymn. We have surely learned from it something of how we ought to pray: with reverence and contrition, with humility and sincerity, with faith and confidence, with patience and courage. What then? The final stanza supplies the answer:

> Give these, and then thy will be done;
>   Thus, strengthened with all might,
> We, through thy Spirit and thy Son,
>   Shall pray, and pray aright.

20.

JESUS OUR FRIEND

What a Friend we have in Jesus
(J. M. Scriven, 1819–86)

The story of this hymn begins in Ireland and ends in Canada. Its author Joseph Scriven, an earnest and dedicated Christian, was an Irishman, born in County Down. He graduated at Trinity College, Dublin, and a happy and useful life seemed to lie before him. But at the age of twenty-five he suffered a terrible loss. The girl he was going to marry was accidentally drowned on the eve of their wedding day, and the young man was overcome with grief. He decided to make a new beginning and emigrate to Canada, where he settled in the province of Ontario and took up teaching.

He wrote the hymn some years later to console his mother on hearing that she was passing through a time of deep sorrow. Not till near the end of his life did the verses come to light. A friend visiting him during his last illness found them by his bedside. 'Did you write these?' he asked Scriven. 'The Lord and I did it between us,' he replied. Clearly it is a hymn born of his personal experience of God's grace. He was no poet and his hymn is not a literary work. Its appeal lies in its simplicity and sincerity and the way it speaks directly to the human heart.

1 A friend for everyone

Plainly the main theme of the hymn is the friendship of Jesus. Strangely enough there are comparatively few hymns that deal with this subject. Perhaps what is even more surprising is that the title 'friend' is never directly given to Jesus in the New

Testament. True, his critics called him 'the friend of sinners', but they did so in contempt and derision because of the disreputable company he kept.

Even so, and however ill meant, the title is true – and gloriously true. Jesus was and is the friend of sinners. His gospel is good news for sinners; and since we are all sinners he is a friend for everyone – and for each one of us here – so that we can sing:

> What a friend *we* have in Jesus,
> All our sins and griefs to bear!

In thinking about this subject let us note that a *friend* differs significantly from a *relation*. We have no choice as regards our kinsfolk, our parents or our brothers and sisters. We are bound to them by blood ties, by birth. But we *are* free to choose our friends. Out of the varied company we meet in life we are drawn to certain people and they to us – perhaps by a sense of affinity, perhaps by common interests. Thus the bond of friendship is formed, a spiritual not a physical bond.

Such is our relationship with the Lord Jesus. We are drawn to him by the magnet of his love and as a result we are bound to him for life. He said to his first disciples, and now says to us, 'You are my friends if you do what I command you' (John 15.14); and since true friendship is mutual we may assuredly call him *our* friend – if we do what he commands us.

2 *A friend in time of need*

We have a saying, 'A friend in need is a friend indeed'. Another proverb says that a friend is never known till he is needed. It is in times of need that we prove the worth of our friends and the quality of their friendship. Our friends certainly mean most to us when things go wrong.

There is an expression we often come across in the Psalms: 'the day of trouble'. Most of us, if not all of us, know something about that day. Joseph Scriven was well acquainted with it and makes repeated reference to it in his hymn. For example:

> Have we trials and temptations?
> Is there trouble anywhere?

Or again:

> Are we weak and heavy-laden,
> Cumbered with a load of care?

The questions ring true to life. So do the allusions to anxiety, discouragement, pain and sorrow. In all such circumstances we find in Jesus a true friend who will never let us down. Indeed,

> Can we find a friend so faithful,
> Who will all our sorrows share?

Not only is he a faithful friend. He is also a sympathetic one, for he shares our sorrows and knows our every weakness.

Again, the hymn raises another question:

> Do thy friends despise, forsake thee?

It is a sad and bitter thing when our friends let us down or break their promises. Yet is happens. The book of Proverbs warns us against 'friends who pretend to be friends', but adds: 'There is a friend who sticks closer than a brother' (18.24). Jesus is just such a friend. Whatever our need, he is always near at hand, always ready to help. As the hymn says,

> In his arms he'll take and shield thee,
> Thou shalt find a solace there.

3 A friend within call

Jesus is a friend always within call. This is the point of the repeated phrase, *Take it to the Lord in prayer*. And this is why Scriven entitled his lines 'Pray without ceasing'.

A human friend cannot be of much help to us if he is far away, out of reach, inaccessible. But Jesus is always accessible, always available. We can come to him at all times, in all places, in all circumstances. That being so,

> What a privilege to carry
> Everything to God in prayer!

Do we sufficiently realize what an immense *privilege* it is to have instant access to the throne of grace? Perhaps we don't always think of prayer in that way. Perhaps we are inclined to look upon it rather as a spiritual chore. But it is more than a religious duty. It is a glorious and unspeakable privilege.

One further question. Do we make a habit of taking *everything* to God in prayer? Nothing is too big to pray about, nothing too small. Our big things are all small to God's power; our little things are all big to his love. If we fail to pray, how much we lose:

> O what peace we often forfeit,
> O what needless pain we bear,
> All because we do not carry
> Everything to God in prayer!

Pray without ceasing. Pray about everything. And pray with confidence, for Jesus is the friend who knows all about us and still remains our friend.

21.

CONVERSION

O happy day that fixed my choice
(P. Doddridge, 1702–51)

John Bunyan, in the introduction to his spiritual autobiography *Grace Abounding to the Chief of Sinners* wrote, 'It is profitable for Christians to be often calling to mind the beginnings of grace with their souls.' This in effect is what Dr Philip Doddridge is doing in this hymn. With wonder and gratitude he is looking back to his conversion, to the time when he first consciously received Christ into his life and confessed him as Lord.

Conversion is not something we normally hear much about from the pulpit, except perhaps around the feast of the Conversion of St Paul (25 January). This hymn at once directs our thoughts to the subject and at the same time helps us to understand what it means. Though the hymn finds a place in all the Free Church hymnals it is not widely known in Anglican circles. Queen Victoria chose it to be sung at the confirmation of one of her daughters. A certain provincial paper in reporting the fact ascribed the authorship of the hymn to Lord Tennyson – and then complained that he wasn't worthy to be Poet Laureate if he couldn't produce something better! Whatever its literary merits the hymn is certainly a spiritual treasure. The jingling chorus sometimes attached to it should be disregarded as having nothing to do with Doddridge's fine work and quite out of keeping with it.

1 A personal decision

What is conversion? The hymn begins by making clear that

conversion involves a personal decision or choice.

> O happy day that fixed my choice
> On thee, my Saviour and my God!
> Well may this glowing heart rejoice,
> And tell its raptures all abroad.

Conversion happens when we personally encounter Jesus Christ – or rather when he encounters us – and we accept him as our Saviour and Lord. He encounters us as he did those first disciples by the Sea of Galilee and says 'Follow me' – and we say 'Yes' to him. He encounters us as he did Saul of Tarsus on the Damascus road and speaks to us by name – and we surrender to his claims.

Conversion can be described in many ways, for the experience differs considerably from person to person. This is what we should expect, for people themselves are different. Yet in every instance of true conversion there is one element in common: a definite *turning* (as the word means) from self to God through Jesus Christ and the acceptance of his salvation.

Conversion then is turning – but not simply turning over a new leaf and living a more moral life. Nor is it turning religious and learning to pray and go to church. There is something else that matters, or rather someone else. The 'happy day' which Doddridge celebrates was the day when he fixed his choice on Christ – 'my Saviour and my God'. It was this that set his heart aglow and made him sing for joy. A new relationship was established between himself and his Lord:

> O happy bond, that seals my vows
> To him who merits all my love;
> Let cheerful anthems fill his house,
> While to that sacred shrine I move.

2 A covenant relationship

So far we have been thinking of conversion from the human

angle. But of course there is another side to it, God's side. And the hymn next brings this side into view:

> 'Tis done, the great transaction's done,
>   I am my Lord's, and he is mine;
> He drew me, and I followed on,
>   Charmed to confess the voice divine.

The word 'transaction' may seem a strange one to use, but it has an important meaning in connection with this subject. A transaction is normally a piece of business which takes place between two persons or parties and the word is used in that sense here. Conversion is a spiritual transaction between ourselves and God through Jesus Christ. The biblical word for it is *covenant*: a solemn agreement entered into between God and man on the basis of mutual promises. God on his part pledges us the grace of his salvation in Christ, and we on ours vow to him our trust and allegiance.

How does it happen? In the words of the hymn, 'He drew me, and I followed on'. The initiative, you will note, lies with the Lord, not with us. It is the love of Christ that draws us to him. We can only love him because he first loved us. We can only give ourselves to him because he first gave himself for us. So conversion, on our side, is essentially a response. It is, as we have emphasized, a *personal* response which each must make for himself or herself. It is also a *free* response, the response of our own wills. And it is a response of *faith*: the trust of the heart as well as the assent of the mind. When we have that sort of faith we also find *peace*, as Doddridge stated in a stanza often omitted:

> Now rest, my long-divided heart,
>   Fixed on this blissful centre, rest:
> With ashes who would grudge to part
>   When called on angels' bread to feast?

Christ is the 'blissful centre' on which our hearts rest, as he is also the 'angels' bread' or manna on which we feed.

85

One further thing we learn about conversion is that it is a life-long commitment. The final stanza makes this clear:

> High heaven, that heard the solemn vow,
> That vow renewed shall daily hear;
> Till in life's latest hour I bow,
> And bless in death a bond so dear.

Conversion is for life. The vow we make to Christ at the outset must be constantly renewed. The bond between ourselves and him must remain unbroken till our dying day.

This means that ultimately what matters is not so much the conversion experience, or when or how it happened. What matters is the genuineness and quality of the converted life as it expresses itself in love to Christ and service to others.

We may not be able to call to mind the beginnings of God's grace with our souls or identify the 'happy day' when we first confessed Jesus as Lord. Our conversion may have been a gradual process, not a sudden crisis. Quite likely we do not know *when* it happened, but we do know – as did Doddridge all those years ago – *what* happened: 'He drew me, and I followed on'. And we know the result: 'I am my Lord's, and he is mine'. That is what matters; and if it is real our life will show it.

22.

FAITH

My faith looks up to thee
(Ray Palmer, 1808–87)

The man who wrote this hymn became one of America's foremost ministers, preachers and hymn-writers. But Ray Palmer had achieved none of these distinctions when he penned 'My faith looks up to thee'. It was written when he was twenty-two, shortly after he had graduated from Yale in 1830. He later recalled that he wrote it with very little effort as a spontaneous expression of his faith and of what Christ meant to him. Having jotted the words down on a slip of paper he slipped it into his pocket book, and there it remained until he happened to meet the American musician Lowell Mason on the street in Boston.

At that time Dr Mason was engaged in compiling a new hymn book and he asked Palmer if he would like to contribute something to it. The young man put his hand in his pocket and produced his hymn. Mason was immediately impressed with the verses, made a copy of them, and when he reached home he composed the tune *Olivet* to which the hymn is nearly always sung. Some days later he met Palmer again and said, 'Mr Palmer, you may live many years and do many good things, but I think you will be best known to posterity as the author of "My faith looks up to thee".' The words proved prophetic to some extent; by Dr Ray Palmer is also remembered now as the author of 'Jesus, thou joy of loving hearts' and 'Jesus, these eyes have never seen', both written some thirty years later. If our present hymn lacks the maturity of those others, it has a freshness and simplicity that is immediately appealing.

1 Faith and consecration

> My faith looks up to thee,
> Thou Lamb of Calvary,
>   Saviour divine!
> Now hear me while I pray,
> Take all my guilt away,
> O let me from this day
>   Be wholly thine.

Faith is the keyword of this hymn. And for Ray Palmer faith was something intensely personal: '*my* faith'. We do not know how or when he came to faith in Christ. He was the son of a judge and grew up in Boston as a member of the Congregational Church. Six years later he wrote the hymn, which when published bore the title 'Self-consecration'.

That note of consecration is sounded in the latter part of the opening stanza. In simple trust the young man is committing his life wholly to the Saviour who died for him, the 'Lamb of Calvary'. In the New Testament Jesus is repeated given the deeply meaningful title of the *lamb* – the emblem of sacrifice. It is especially prominent in the book of Revelation, where we catch a vision of Christ as the lamb slain for the redemption of mankind, worshipped and adored by the whole company of heaven.

We who are members of the Church on earth are one in this respect with the Church triumphant above. We glory in the cross. We worship the crucified Saviour; and we do this more especially in the Eucharist. As we offer him our praise and thanksgiving we also consecrate our lives to him afresh – 'our souls and bodies, to be a living sacrifice'. The faith in which we first committed ourselves to Christ must be constantly renewed and expressed in holy, dedicated lives.

2 Faith and service

When as a young man Ray Palmer wrote this hymn he had the sense to realize that the life on which he was embarking would not be an easy one. As a minister of the gospel a lot would be expected of him, a lot demanded. 'Who is sufficient for these things?' he may well have asked himself; and with that question in mind he prayed:

> May thy rich grace impart
> Strength to my fainting heart,
>   My zeal inspire;
> As thou hast died for me,
> O may my love for thee
> Pure, warm, and changeless be,
>   A living fire.

Young as he was at the time, in the full vigour of his physical and mental powers, Ray Palmer knew better than to rely on his own strength in his life of service. He was aware of his inner weakness. He speaks of his 'fainting heart'. Wisely then he seeks the riches of God's grace to sustain him and kindle his zeal. What if he should lose his early enthusiasm for the Lord's work? Worse still, what if his burning love for the Christ who had died for him were to grow cold?

The risen Lord's charge against the church at Ephesus was that it had abandoned its first love for him; and his charge against the church at Laodicea was that it was merely luke-warm (Rev.2.4; 3.16). It is a sad thing when devotion to Christ flags. Palmer recognizes the peril and prays that, far from growing cold, his love might always be 'warm' – yes, and more than warm, 'a living fire'!

3 Faith and the future

In the two final stanzas the writer looks to the future. He does not know what lies ahead, so he asks the Lord to be his guide as he treads 'life's dark maze'. And life does sometimes seem like that. Again, there may be sorrows as well as joys ahead, dark days as well as bright ones, and temptations of all kinds to be met with. We all know these things; and therefore we may well pray, as the third stanza teaches us to do, that the Lord will illuminate our path, console our sorrows, and always keep us close to himself.

The final stanza looks farther ahead still.

> When ends life's transient dream,
> When death's cold sullen stream
> > Shall o'er me roll,
> Blest Saviour, then in love
> Fear and distrust remove;
> O bear me safe above,
> > A ransomed soul.

It may seem strange that a young man, at the beginning of his life, should so soon be thinking about its end. But here Ray Palmer was simply following a pattern set by the evangelical hymn-writers of his day. They felt that a hymn was not complete unless it finished with an allusion to death and the life beyond. He was dutifully adhering to the tradition.

The Victorians were less inhibited about death than we are. They were also more interested in heaven than ourselves. Perhaps we have something to learn from them. At any rate it is unrealistic to ignore the fact of death, and unchristian to lose sight of heaven. And our faith should enable us to face the one fearlessly and the other joyfully.

23.

PROMISES

O Jesus, I have promised
(J. E. Bode, 1816–74)

The Reverend John Bode, the author of this hymn, must be numbered among the large company of 'one hymn' writers: that is, hymn-writers who are now remembered by a single composition. He was a scholarly man and published two or three volumes of verse, but of all he wrote this hymn is the sole survivor.

He wrote it about the year 1866, for the confirmation of his own children. It is an excellent Confirmation hymn, though in fact it makes no direct or explicit mention of Confirmation. But this fault, if it is a fault, gives the hymn a wider appeal and doubtless accounts for the fact that, well over a century after it was written, it is now used throughout the world in churches of all communions.

What is the hymn about? Three things in particular: the promises we make as Christian disciples; the perils that beset us in daily life; and the Lord's unfailing presence with us to the end.

1 The Christian's promise

To begin with, the hymn is about promises, especially those which we make to Jesus. The opening words provide the key:

> O Jesus, I have promised
> To serve thee to the end.

Confirmation, as we know, has two sides, God's side and

ours. What God does on his side is to confirm or strengthen us by his Holy Spirit. What we do on our side is to confirm or ratify our baptismal vows and make them our own. This hymn is concerned primarily with *our* side and the promises we make. What are those promises?

In essence they involve two things, repentance and faith: renunciation of the world, the flesh and the devil, and belief in God the Father, the Son, and the Holy Spirit. Those promises are not peculiar to confirmation. They are the promises required of all who profess and call themselves Christians of whatever persuasion.

The hymn sums them up in the simple phrase 'to serve thee to the end'. To *serve* Christ involves trust, loyalty, obedience, dedication. To serve him *to the end* means that the promises are for life. So also is Confirmation. The whole thing is not over when the service is finished. That is merely the beginning. We pledge ourselves to serve Christ all our days, not only at the start but to the end of life.

Such promises are more easily made than kept. The path of discipleship is a hard and difficult one. The hymn warns us about that.

2 *The perils of discipleship*

There is some plain speaking about the perils of the Christian life. The world in which we seek to serve our Lord is not a comfortable place for those who take their vows seriously and try to be faithful. The hymn views the world as a Vanity Fair for the Christian pilgrim. The second stanza begins:

> O let me feel thee near me:
> The world is ever near:
> I see the sights that dazzle,
> The tempting sounds I here.

The 'world' here means the secular world, the godless world,

92

with its 'sights that dazzle' and its 'tempting sounds'. Exactly what form those sights and sounds took over a century ago when this hymn was written we can only guess. What they are today we know well enough. Life for a loyal Christian, especially a young Christian, is bound to be a spiritual struggle in a largely pagan society which has banished God and has no time or place for him.

But more. The stanza goes on to remind us that our foes are not only 'around' us but also 'within' – inherent in our sinful nature and our weak, wayward wills. So we pray:

> O let me hear thee speaking
> In accents clear and still,
> Above the storms of passion,
> The murmurs of self-will.

The word 'passion' reminds us of our sensuality and of the battle for purity and honour we all have to face. We can hardly expect to escape it in this sex-ridden age. We know something of that inner conflict which St Paul described when he wrote: 'The desires of the flesh are against the Spirit, and the desires of the Spirit are against the flesh, and these are opposed to one another' (Gal.5.17).

Temptation is an inescapable fact of life. It takes different forms for different people and Christians are certainly not exempt. We are all vulnerable and the devil knows our weakest points. How can we be victorious? The hymn has an answer to the question.

3 The presence of the Lord

Running all through the stanzas in the assurance of the Lord's unfailing presence with us in life's battle. In the first stanza we sing:

> Be thou for ever near me,
> My Master and my Friend;

I shall not fear the battle
If thou art by my side. . .

The next stanza begins with the prayer 'O let me feel thee near me' and ends, after referring to the nearness of our foes,

But Jesus, draw thou nearer,
And shield my soul from sin.

In Confirmation, as we said at the beginning, God confirms or strengthens us by his Holy Spirit. This hymn makes no reference to the gift of the Spirit. It speaks instead of the presence of the living Christ. Is there some confusion or contradiction here?

No, for in actual experience there is no difference. The Holy Spirit is the Spirit of Christ, Christ's other self, Christ in us. That is why the New Testament sometimes speaks of the *Spirit*, sometimes of *Christ*, dwelling in us. The terms are interchangeable. Jesus promised his disciples that in the coming of the Spirit he himself would come to them (John 14.18). He also promised them at the last, 'Surely I will be with you to the end of the age' (Matt.28.20). And he *is* with us now – by his Spirit.

In his confirmation hymn John Bode chose to speak of the indwelling Christ rather than of the indwelling Spirit. This is easier for children to grasp. The whole hymn is consistently Christ-centred. Note the titles by which he is addressed; and then note how the prayer in the final stanza sums up the hymn's entire message:

O let me see thy footmarks,
And in them plant mine own;
My hope to follow duly
Is in thy strength alone;
O guide me, call me, draw me,
Uphold me to the end;
And then in heaven receive me,
My Saviour and my Friend.

24.

WALKING WITH GOD

O for a closer walk with God
(W. Cowper, 1731–1800)

The poet William Cowper wrote this hymn on 9 December 1769. We know the exact date from a letter he wrote to a friend the following day. In this he referred to the serious illness of his faithful friend and housekeeper Mrs Unwin. 'Her illness has been a sharp trial to me,' he said. 'Oh that it may have a sanctified effect, that I may rejoice to surrender up to the Lord my dearest comforts the moment he may require them.'

It was something of a spiritual crisis in Cowper's life. He had come to rely so entirely on Mrs Unwin's help and support. What if she were to be taken from him? How could he manage without her? This is the background to the hymn. It reflects the poet's troubled state of mind, as also his highly sensitive nature and introspective religious outlook, as do many of his other hymns.

1 Aspiration

The hymn strikes four different notes, beginning with *aspiration.*

> O for a closer walk with God,
> A calm and heavenly frame;
> A light to shine upon the road
> That leads me to the Lamb!

Cowper entitled the hymn 'Walking with God' and the Bible reference he attached to it was Genesis 5.24: 'Enoch walked

95

with God, and he was not, for God took him.' He yearned for a *closer* walk with God because he evidently felt that his anxieties and fears were due to his being in some way out of touch with the Lord. Only by getting nearer to him could he find 'a calm and heavenly frame'.

Throughout his life that was the one thing he most lacked and most desired. He constantly suffered from fits of deep depression and religious melancholy. Instead of walking in the light he stumbled along in a state of spiritual darkness. He acknowledged it only too readily. Hence his further longing for 'a light to shine upon the road': a light that would dispel the darkness and direct his steps straight to Christ.

2 Recollection

The next note struck is that of *recollection*. Cowper looks back on his spiritual pilgrimage and asks somewhat wistfully:

> Where is the blessedness I knew
> When first I saw the Lord?
> Where is the soul-refreshing view
> Of Jesus and his word?

The poet is here referring to the evangelical conversion he had experienced some six years earlier. After a severe mental breakdown he had been sent by his friends to a private asylum at St Albans run by a Dr Cotton, a wise and kindly Christian man. Under his care and counselling Cowper gradually recovered his sanity. At the same time, through reading the scriptures, he came to a personal faith in Christ as his saviour and as a result he found – for a time, at any rate – true peace of heart.

Now he remembers that time. How clear *then* had been his vision of the Lord! What precious truths he had discovered in the Bible! So he continues:

What peaceful hours I once enjoyed!
    How sweet their memory still!
But they have left an aching void
    The world can never fill.

Those 'peaceful hours' were now no more than a tantalizing memory. The 'blessedness' of past years had departed. Once again he was in a disturbed mental state. His heart was 'an aching void' and nothing that the world had to offer could satisfy him.

There is something very sad about these two stanzas. It is not surprising that many hymn books omit them, for admittedly they do not represent a normal or healthy state for the Christian believer. Yet if we are honest must we not agree that the words strike a realistic note? Do they not answer to something that many of us know to be only too true in our spiritual history? Even so, Cowper's words are more suitable to reflect on in private than to sing in public worship. And the same could be said of certain stanzas in many other hymns.

3 Penitence

What next? Quite rightly the poet does not simply brood over his loss of faith, his low religious condition. He prays, and prays earnestly and with deep penitence:

Return, O holy Dove, return,
    Sweet messenger of rest;
I hate the sins that made thee mourn,
    And drove thee from by breast.

The prayer is addressed to the Holy Spirit under the symbolism of the dove, the symbol used in the account of our Lord's baptism. Cowper felt that by his 'sins' – perhaps more imaginary than real – he had 'grieved the Holy Spirit of God' (Ephesians 4.30). Doubtless we ourselves often do the same by our disobedience to God's will and so rob ourselves of the sense of his presence. True penitence means not only renouncing sin but recognizing God's sole sovereignty:

> The dearest idol I have known,
>   Whate'er that idol be,
> Help me to tear it from thy throne,
>   And worship only thee.

What is an idol? Anything that usurps the place of God in our lives and becomes the primary object of our worship. People can, and often do, make an idol of money, pleasure, possessions, fame, success. These are false gods. And however dear, they must be dethroned. 'Guard yourselves from idols', wrote the apostle John (1 John 5.21). And Jesus answered Satan in the wilderness with the words, 'You shall worship the Lord your God and him only shall you serve.'

4 Assurance

Note how the hymn ends. With sin renounced and God enthroned it reaches the logical conclusion:

> So shall my walk be close with God,
>   Calm and serene my frame;
> So purer light shall mark the road
>   That leads me to the Lamb.

The language of this final stanza is very similar to that of the first, yet it is significantly different. While for the most part the same words are repeated, there is a subtle change of mood. At the beginning the mood was that of aspiration. Now aspiration gives place to *assurance*. 'So *shall* my walk be close with God . . . So purer light *shall* mark the road . . .' Prayer has prevailed. Doubt has vanished. Faith has triumphed. We are left with a picture of the believer's life as it should be: fully surrendered to God and ruled by the peace of Christ.

25.

SANCTIFICATION

Love divine, all loves excelling
(Charles Wesley, 1707–88)

This hymn – one of the great favourites among Charles Wesley's vast output – has a curious history. He got the idea of writing it from a popular song of the day, the 'Song of Venus' in Dryden's play *King Arthur*, set to music by Henry Purcell. The song began:

> Fairest isle, all isles excelling,
> Seat of pleasure and of loves,
> Venus here will choose her dwelling,
> And forsake her Cyprian groves.

Probably it was not so much the words as the entrancing tune that first captured Wesley's attention. At any rate he wrote the hymn in the same metre and it was originally sung to Purcell's melody. But clearly the amorous words of the song also suggested the theme of the hymn, divine love – a love far excelling that of a pagan goddess; and thus our hymn was fashioned.

1 The love of Christ

It begins accordingly by celebrating the love of Christ. He himself is the 'Love divine' to whom the hymn is addressed. His love so far exceeds all other loves that its length and breadth, its height and depth, are immeasurable. It is love that surpasses human knowledge (Eph.3.18). So Wesley writes:

> Jesu, thou art all compassion,
>> Pure, unbounded love thou art.

Wesley is always at his best when writing of the love of Christ, God's love incarnate. This is hardly surprising since the words of scripture that gripped him at the crisis of his conversion in May 1738 were: 'The Son of God loved me, and gave himself for me' (Gal.2.20). For him the cross was the proof and pledge of that 'pure, unbounded love'. He longed to know more of what Christ had done for him and to be wholly absorbed in his love. Hence in another of his hymns written a year or two later he cried,

> O Love divine, how sweet thou art!
> When shall I find my willing heart
>> All taken up by thee?
> I thirst, I faint, I die to prove
> The greatness of redeeming love,
>> The love of Christ to me.

2 The sanctuary of the heart

The burden of Wesley's prayer in the present hymn is for the indwelling presence of Christ in all his boundless love. That prayer has already been expressed in the opening words,

> Joy of heaven, to earth come down.

And by this he means 'Come down and dwell in our lives'. Hence

> Fix in us thy humble dwelling,

and again,

> Visit us with thy salvation,
>> Enter every trembling heart.

Clearly Wesley has in mind Paul's prayer for his readers in Ephesus: 'that Christ may dwell in your hearts by faith' (3.17). This thought is developed in the second stanza:

> Come, almighty to deliver,
>> Let us all thy grace receive;
> Suddenly return, and never,
>> Never more thy temples leave.

Here the poet is thinking of the words of the prophet Malachi: 'The Lord, whom ye seek, shall suddenly come to his temple' (3.1). He is thinking too of the apostle's words to the Corinthians, 'Do you not know that you are God's temple?' (1 Cor.3.16). St Peter pictures the whole Church as being 'a spiritual house' or temple, of which believers are 'living stones'; and then by a swift transition of thought he sees them as 'a holy priesthood' serving within the temple and offering 'spiritual sacrifices acceptable to God through Jesus Christ' (1 Pet.2.5,6). These spiritual sacrifices are also referred to in the hymn:

> Thee we would be always blessing,
>> Serve thee as thy hosts above,
> Pray, and praise thee, without ceasing,
>> Glory in thy perfect love.

3 The way of holiness

In the final stanza Wesley turns from the thought of service to that of sanctification:

> Finish then thy new creation,
>> Pure and spotless let us be.

We who are 'in Christ' are his 'new creation' (2 Cor.5.17); and our prayer is that he will finish the good work he has begun in us (Phil.1.6) and sanctify us wholly. We are not to be content with half measures. God is faithful and just not only to *forgive* us our sins but 'to *cleanse* us from all unrighteousness' (1 John 1.9). So we pray that we may be 'pure and spotless'.

It is known that what Charles Wesley originally wrote was 'pure and *sinless* let us be'. His brother John changed the word to avoid suggesting the false idea of sinless perfection. But both men were fully persuaded that God's 'great salvation' was sufficient to deliver the believer from the *power* as well as from the guilt of sin and so enable him to lead a pure, strong and holy life. They accepted the teaching of the apostle John: 'No one who is born of God will continue to sin', that is, continue to lead a sinful life (1 John 3.9). The prayer in the *Te Deum* is in accordance with this: 'Vouchsafe, O Lord, to keep us this day without sin'.

In another of his hymns Wesley prayed for 'a heart from sin set free' – and more still:

> A heart in every thought renewed,
>   And full of love divine,
> Perfect, and right, and pure, and good,
>   A copy, Lord, of thine.

To be holy in this way is not a human achievement. It is God's progressive work in the soul through the indwelling presence of Christ in the Spirit. And thus we are being *changed*:

> Changed from glory into glory,
>   Till in heaven we take our place,
> Till we cast our crowns before thee,
>   Lost in wonder, love, and praise!

Commenting on these words Dr Erik Routley observed, 'This is sanctification, the changing from glory into glory, the increasing of the power to absorb for oneself and reflect for the world the glory and brightness of the character of Christ.'

26.

CHRIST IS ALL

Fight the good fight with all thy might
(J. S. B. Monsell, 1811–75)

The author of this popular hymn, John Samuel Bewley Monsell (to give him his full name) wrote nearly three hundred hymns in all. Many of them were once well known; now only two find a regular place in our hymn books, this one and the Epiphany hymn, 'O worship the Lord in the beauty of holiness'.

Monsell does not rank as one of the leading English hymn-writers. But we must be grateful for these two hymns, and we should surely agree that he had the right idea when he declared that his intention was to make hymns 'more fervent and joyous'. Victorian hymns, the hymns of his day, tended to be excessively subjective and morbid, inward-looking and preoccupied with death and the hereafter. Monsell's hymns strike a healthier and happier note. He was an Irishman whose father was Archdeacon of Londonderry. He began his own ministry in Ireland but moved to England some twenty years later to be vicar of Egham, Surrey. He was later appointed rector of St Nicholas, Guildford, where he died tragically at the age of sixty-four as the result of an accident during the rebuilding of his church.

'Fight the good fight' is the hymn by which he is best remembered. What sort of hymn is it?

1 A hymn of faith

The title it was originally given, 'The Fight for Faith', and its opening line might suggest that it is a Christian battle song like 'Onward, Christian soldiers'. But this is not so. The rest of the hymn has nothing to say about fighting. The one word in the title which is wholly relevant is the word *faith*. The hymn is essentially a hymn of faith: faith in its various aspects and pre-eminently faith in Christ. It is a thoroughly biblical hymn and its material is derived almost entirely from the New Testament epistles.

Consider the first stanza.

> Fight the good fight with all thy might,
> Christ is thy strength and Christ thy right;
> Lay hold on life, and it shall be
> Thy joy and crown eternally.

Some words of St Paul to Timothy inspired these lines: 'Fight the good fight of faith, lay hold on eternal life' (1 Tim.6.12). And the apostle's own final testimony was, 'I have fought a good fight; I have finished the course; I have kept the faith' (2 Tim.4.7). Clearly the 'fight' he had in mind was the fight for *the* faith, that is, the faith of the gospel. Paul had been engaged in that struggle throughout his ministry and now he is urging Timothy to continue it.

But in this hymn Monsell is not thinking of that sort of fight. He wrote it for the nineteenth Sunday after Trinity, the Epistle of which in the *BCP* (Eph.4.17–32) is all about Christian conduct; abandoning the old pagan way of life and walking 'in righteousness and true holiness'. The fight in question, then, is the fight *against* sin, the fight *for* sanctity. And this is something which concerns us all. We may not be called or qualified to defend the Christian faith, but we certainly are called to maintain and exemplify the Christian way of life. In godless days like these it is a hard and costly struggle, but we are not left to our own resources. Christ is our strength and he is with us in the battle.

2 Christ the object of faith

In the second stanza the metaphor changes:

> Run the straight race through God's good grace,
> Lift up thine eyes, and seek his face;
> Life with its way before us lies,
> Christ is the path, and Christ the prize.

The Christian life is now viewed as an athletic contest and again the imagery is borrowed from the epistles. Says the writer to the Hebrews, 'Let us run with perseverance the race that is set before us, looking unto Jesus . . .' (Heb.12.1,2). Christ is the object of faith. 'Lift up thine eyes and seek *his* face'! Christian faith is emphatically faith in Christ. That is why this hymn, so full of faith, is also so full of Christ.

Some words of St Paul also find an echo in this stanza: 'I press on towards the goal to win the prize of the upward call of God in Christ Jesus' (Phil.3.14). Christ is both the *path*, setting the direction in which we are to run, and the *prize* awaiting us at the end of the race. In Christ, life is purposeful and progressive. 'Through God's good grace' let us press on and never give up.

3 The victories of faith

The last two stanzas deal with the victories of faith in our daily lives. For one thing, faith conquers our cares:

> Cast care aside, upon thy Guide
> Lean, and his mercy will provide;
> Lean, and the trusting soul shall prove
> Christ is its life, and Christ its love.

Monsell had in mind here the words of the apostle Peter, 'Casting all your care upon him (the Lord), for he careth for you' (1 Pet.5.7). The word rendered 'care' in the *AV* is rightly translated 'anxiety' in modern versions. Life at times can be a very anxious, worrying affair. What are we to do? 'Cast thy burden upon the Lord', says the psalmist' – and so does the hymn. 'Lean on thy Guide'! Yes, *lean*: the word is repeated. To lean is to rely, and this is the attitude of 'the trusting soul'.

The last verse continues the theme of victorious faith:

> Faint not nor fear, his arms are near,
> He changeth not, and thou are dear;
> Only believe, and thou shalt see
> That Christ is all in all to thee.

Christ is near us; he is unchanging and unchangeable; and he loves us dearly. These are the convictions that banish fear and bring peace to the trusting soul. *Only believe*! Faith is the great requisite on the human side, for it is by faith we discover in actual experience that 'Christ is all in all' to us.

As we look back over the hymn we see that its Christ-centredness is really its distinctive and dominant feature. The strong imperatives that ring out in verse after verse would be utterly futile apart from Christ. We can only fight the good fight if Christ is our strength. We can only run the straight race if Christ is the path we follow. We can only overcome our cares and our fears if Christ is the guide on whom we lean.

'Christ is all' (Col.3.11) – or as Moffatt renders it, 'Christ is everything'. That is the message of the hymn to treasure and take away with you.

27.

DISCIPLESHIP

Jesus calls us! O'er the tumult
(Mrs C. F. Alexander, 1818–95)

The Irish hymn-writer, Mrs Cecil Frances Alexander, is known chiefly for her children's hymns, such as 'All things bright and beautiful' and 'There is a green hill far away'[see no. 11]. These were among her earliest hymns, published shortly before her marriage to the Reverend William Alexander in 1850. She continued to write hymns throughout her life, many of them for particular festivals and saints' days. One of the most familiar is her hymn for Trinity Sunday, known as St Patrick's Breastplate, 'I bind unto myself today'. But better known still is her hymn for St Andrew's Day (30 November) – 'Jesus calls us', a hymn with a universal appeal and which can be sung throughout the year.

It is based on the opening words of the Gospel for St Andrew's Day in the BCP, Mathew 4.18–20:

As Jesus walked by the Sea of Galilee, he saw two brothers, Simon who is called Peter and Andrew his brother, casting a net into the sea, for they were fishermen. And he said to them, 'Follow me, and I will make you fishers of men.' Immediately they left their nets and followed him.

1 The invitation to follow

With those words in mind we turn to the hymn. It begins:

Jesus calls us! O'er the tumult
Of our life's wild restless sea,

Day by day his sweet voice soundeth,
    Saying, 'Christian, follow me.'

The theme throughout the hymn is the *call* of Jesus. The word occurs in almost every verse. And the call consists basically of just those two words, 'Follow me'. That same call is heard again and again in the Gospels. Brief though it is, the call is full of meaning and is worth thinking about.

What is implied in 'following' Jesus? For one thing it involves commitment. A follower is an adherent. When Jesus says 'Follow me' he means in effect, 'Throw in your lot with me; give me your personal, wholehearted allegiance.' And that – as the hymn makes clear – is what he is still saying to us today.

Again, to follow someone in the literal sense involves keeping close to that person, so as not to lose contact with him. The same is true of following Jesus. We must keep close to him. We must walk daily in his company. We must never lose sight of him or get out of touch.

One other thing. Following Jesus implies copying him: what Thomas à Kempis called *The Imitation of Christ*. He has left us an example that we should follow in his steps (1 Pet.2.21). The outcome of this will be becoming more like him, adopting his way of life, reflecting something of his love.

Jesus calls us. The initiative is with him, not with us. He takes the first step. Long before we seek him we may be sure that the Lord is seeking us, calling us in the midst of 'our life's wild restless sea'. The words convey a picture of the Sea of Galilee swept by a sudden storm. It is intended to be a picture of our own restless lives before Christ meets with us and calls us to follow him. Then it is with us as it was with the apostles those centuries ago:

    As of old St Andrew heard it
        By the Galilean lake,
    Turned from home, and toil, and kindred,
        Leaving all for his dear sake.

That day the fishermen brothers were confronted with a choice. It was not a command but an invitation that Jesus gave them. There was no compulsion. They were free agents, free to ignore the call altogether if they desired; free to say 'Yes' and equally free to say 'No'. Jesus was looking not for conscripts but for willing followers – just as he is today.

In the case of Andrew and Peter the answer was clear and immediate. They had already been attracted to Jesus as they listened to his teaching and watched him at work. Now their minds were made up. But it was a costly decision. It meant the renunciation of their old life, turning their backs upon 'home, and toil, and kindred, leaving all for his dear sake'.

Jesus claims the total allegiance of his followers, now as then.

> Jesus calls us from the worship
> Of the vain world's golden store,
> From each idol that would keep us,
> Saying, 'Christian, love me more.'

Jesus calls us *from* the love of the world *to* a wholehearted love for him. He must be our first love. Anything else is an idol; and certainly the biggest idol that claims our worship, as the hymn indicates, is money – 'the vain world's golden store'. Of course money itself is not an evil, but the love of money – that is, making a god of money – certainly is, an evil that all too readily usurps the place of Christ in our lives.

There are other things too that may come between us and our Lord, as the next stanza (v.4) indicates. It reminds us of the lesser idols that threaten our devotion to Christ: our work, our pleasures, our leisure activities (e.g. our hobbies), along with our cares and sorrows. Whatever claims such things make upon us, the Lord is saying, 'Christian, love me *more* than these.'

The call of Jesus requires a response from us as surely as it did from those of old. The final stanza puts it in the form of a prayer:

> Jesus calls us! By thy mercies,
>   Saviour, may we hear thy call,
> Give our hearts to thy obedience,
>   Serve and love thee best of all.

Our prayer is that by the Lord's 'mercies' – that is, by his grace and aid – we may not only hear but heed his call. And that will involve three things: yielding to him the obedience of our hearts, serving him gladly all our days, and loving him more than anything else in life.

It is a prayer of consecration. We should not take the words lightly upon our lips. Indeed, we ought not to sing them at all unless we really mean what we are saying.

28.

SUFFERING

O Love that wilt not let me go
(George Matheson, 1842–1906)

A romantic story used to be told about the origin of this hymn by George Matheson, a distinguished minister of the Scottish Church. From childhood he had suffered from poor eyesight and by his eighteenth year he was practically blind. Nothing, he was assured, could be done to save his sight. When (so the story goes) he announced the tragic news to the girl he had hoped to marry, she broke off the engagement; and that same night, in his bitter grief and disappointment, he wrote the hymn about the love that would not let him go.

It is a good story, but in fact pure legend. The hymn was not written in Matheson's youth but many years later when he was forty years of age. He himself left on record an account of how it came about.

The hymn was composed in the manse of Innellan on the evening of 6 June, 1882. I was at that time alone. Something had happened to me which was known only to myself and which caused me the most severe mental suffering. The hymn was the fruit of that suffering. It was the quickest bit of work I ever did in my life. I am quite sure the whole work was completed in five minutes. I had the impression of having it dictated to me by some inward voice.

We do not know what caused Matheson his severe mental distress. But what stands out in his account is that the hymn was the fruit of *suffering* – and this is the key to its meaning. Suffering is its theme throughout. The language is by no means simple or straightforward. A strong mystical strain runs through it and this makes it all the more difficult to understand. Let us look at the four stanzas in turn and seek to elucidate their message.

1 The Love that holds us

Remember, here is a man in great spiritual distress seeking comfort and relief. His own inner resources are inadequate. Human help is of no avail. He turns in desperation to God and in an act of total surrender throws himself into the arms of divine love.

> O Love that wilt not let me go,
>   I rest my weary soul in thee;
>   I give thee back the life I owe,

That in thine ocean depths its flow
May richer, fuller be.

We can understand fairly well what these words meant to George Matheson when he wrote them. Have they any application to ourselves? Most certainly. The love that holds us and will never let us go is the love of God. In that love alone lies our eternal security. No one can pluck us from the Father's hand (John 10.29). In complete confidence we can *rest* our souls in him. But at the same time we acknowledge the total claim his love has upon us and yield our lives back to him: the lives he has created, the lives he has redeemed, the lives which therefore we owe to him. And the wonderful thing is that in thus *giving* ourselves to God we *receive* more than we give. Submerged as it were in the 'ocean depth' of his love, our lives become immeasurably richer, more complete, liberated from the things of earth and exalted to a new spiritual level.

2 *The Light that follows us*

O Light that followest all my way,
I yield my flickering torch to thee.

In singing those words we may remember that the man who wrote them was blind and lived in a world of darkness. But here he is not referring to light or sight in the physical sense. His eyes were blind, but his soul was not in the dark. The light of divine truth had followed him all his way in life; hence his reference to his 'flickering torch', by which he means the measure of inner light he had so far received. But he longs for greater spiritual illumination, with the result that he is now yielding his light, as before he had yielded his life, back to God – and with the same general aim in view:

My heart restores its borrowed ray,
That in thy sunshine's blaze its day
May brighter, fairer be.

You can see his meaning. He is offering to God the light already granted to him (the 'borrowed ray') in order that in the blazing sunshine of heaven it may become all the brighter. In effect, then, this is a prayer for a clearer knowledge of God, who is eternal light and in whom is no darkness at all (1 John 1.5).

3 *The Joy that seeks us*

Note carefully the opening lines of the third stanza:

> O Joy that seekest me through pain,
> I cannot close my heart to thee.

Is it true that God, who is now personified as joy, seeks us through the medium of pain and suffering? Pain is not normally associated with joy. Yet if in time of mental or physical anguish we are prepared to open our hearts to God and allow him to come in, we may find that he brings us a joy and peace which the world cannot give. Surely this has been the experience of many of God's people in every age.

This is the basic meaning of the lines that follow:

> I trace the rainbow through the rain,
> And feel the promise is not vain,
> That morn shall tearless be.

The language of course is symbolical, derived from the story of the flood. God gave Noah the rainbow as a shining emblem of *hope*, with the promise that never again would rain destroy the earth (Gen.9.12–17). So here *rain* represents the element of affliction; and the words come to mean that in our troubles and trials we may continue to exercise hope and to believe God's promise of a 'tearless' morning – that is a morning of joy. And so the stanza ends on the same note with which it begins. (Cf. Psalm 30.5.)

113

4 The Cross that raises us

The final verse points us to the cross: the cross as a sign not only of suffering but of sacrifice:

> O Cross that liftest up my head,
>   I dare not ask to fly from thee;
> I lay in dust life's glory dead,
> And from the ground there blossoms red
>   Life that shall endless be.

Dr Matheson himself explained what he meant by the phrase 'blossoms red'. White blossoms, he said, represent prosperity; red ones portray self-sacrifice. 'I took red as the symbol of that sacrificial life which blooms by shedding itself.'

As Christians we 'dare not', as the hymn says, shirk the sacrificial life. We identify ourselves with the cross. The cross is the pattern of our discipleship. And the eventual result is not loss but gain. We die to live. For as Jesus said, 'Whoever would save his life will lose it; and whoever loses his life for my sake and the gospel's will save it' (Mark 8.35).

The tune generally associated with this hymn, *St Margaret*, was composed for it by Dr Albert Peace, organist of Glasgow Cathedral. Like the hymn, the tune was a work of sudden inspiration. After carefully reading the words, says Dr Peace, he wrote the music straight off; 'and I may say that the ink of the first note was hardly dry when I had finished the tune.'

29.

GUIDANCE

Lead, kindly Light, amid the encircling gloom
(J. H. Newman, 1801–90)

The little orange-boat making for Marseilles lay becalmed for a whole week in the Mediterranean in that summer of 1833. On board was a young clergyman, John Henry Newman, vicar of St Mary's, Oxford. After a visit to the continent he was impatiently making his way back to England – physically weak as a result of a serious bout of fever, and inwardly torn by deep religious questions affecting his future. Later he recalled that anxious voyage and wrote in his *Apologia*:

'We were becalmed for a whole week in the Straits of Bonifacio, and it was there that I wrote the lines "Lead, kindly Light" which have since become so well known.'

The lines belong to Newman's own inner history. They are a fragment of his spiritual autobiography. He had not intended them to be a hymn and questioned their suitability for singing. But when many years later Dr J. B. Dykes composed his tune *Lux Benigna* for the words they quickly became exceedingly popular and found a place in all the hymnals.

The three stanzas look in three different directions. The first is concerned with the *present*, the second with the *past*, and the third with the *future*. And each strikes a distinctive note: the first that of *faith*, the second of *penitence*, the third of *hope*.

1 The present: a prayer of faith

When Newman published his poem in 1834, he entitled it 'The Pillar of Cloud'. Plainly he was thinking of the Israelites'

journey through the wilderness when God guided their way to
the promised land by a pillar of cloud and fire (Ex.13.21). This
is the imagery that lies behind the first stanza:

> Lead, kindly Light, amid the encircling gloom,
>   Lead thou me on;
> The night is dark, and I am far from home,
>   Lead thou me on.

When he wrote the words Newman felt like a man on a
journey overtaken by darkness and uncertain of his bearings.
He wanted to be sure he was going in the right direction. He
longed for a gleam of light on his path. So he looked to God for
guidance and prayed 'Lead thou me on'. In one form or
another the phrase is repeated several times and becomes a sort
of refrain. The prayer continues:

> Keep thou my feet; I do not ask to see
> The distant scene: one step enough for me.

The two lines breathe the spirit of quiet trust. Though he
does not know the way, this man is sure of his guide. The hand
that holds him will not fail. He knows too that it is not 'the
distant scene' that matters, only the next step. That is always so
in life's journey. God guides his people a step at a time – if only
they have faith to follow. And in seeking his direction we must
sometimes look *down* as well as look *up*.

2 The past: an act of penitence

In the second verse Newman looks to the past and recalls with
shame how stubborn and self-willed he had been in his early
years. In his *Apologia* he makes repeated reference to the fact
that as a youth he had drifted through life without any true
faith or sense of purpose. 'I had formed no religious convictions till I was fifteen,' he wrote. And in his private diary he
admitted to having been proud, arrogant and bad-tempered,

116

especially in his relations with his parents. Now therefore penitence blends with prayer as he confesses:

> I was not ever thus, nor prayed that thou
>   Shouldst lead me on;
> I loved to choose and see my path; but now
>   Lead thou me on.

But now! There had come a turning point in Newman's life when he experienced the transforming grace of God. As a result everything was different. His scale of values changed. Before, as he says,

> I loved the garish day, and spite of fears
> Pride ruled my will: remember not past years.

By the 'garish day' he means the gaudy, glittering things of the world. Such things attracted him no longer. 'Pride ruled my will' – he admits it. He had wished to be his own master, to run his own life. But now self had been dethroned and his life had found a new centre in the will of God. Well might he pray, 'remember not past years'.

This part of the poem is deeply introspective and represents an honest bit of soul-searching. There is a time and place for that in all our lives. But we must not indulge in it too often or for too long. We must take our eyes off ourselves and get them fixed on God. We must forget the past and look to the future. And this is what Newman does in his final stanza.

3 The future: an affirmation of hope

> So long thy power hath blest me, sure it still
>   Will lead me on
> O'er moor and fen, o'er crag and torrent, till
>   The night is gone.

The writer's confidence as he looks ahead rests on what God

117

has already done for him. 'So long thy power hath blest me', he gratefully testifies; and he is certain that the same divine power will continue to lead him on, whatever path he must tread. 'Moor and fen' represents the easier, more ordinary side of life when things go smoothly. On the other hand, 'crag and torrent' portrays a different aspect when difficulties and dangers are to be encountered. We do not choose our path in life. We leave that to God, for he knows best. All we ask is that he will go ahead and lead the way 'till the night is gone':

> And with the morn those angel faces smile,
> Which I have loved long since, and lost a while.

What is the meaning of these last two lines? Newman, when asked that question near the end of his life, replied that after nearly fifty years he could not remember what had been in his mind when he wrote the words.

Many answers have been suggested, some highly fanciful and unconvincing. Undoubtedly most of us when we sing the words think that the smiling angel faces are loved ones in heaven with whom, after life's short parting, we shall at last be reunited. It is by no means certain that this is what Newman meant; but, as it has been said, in using this hymn each one of us must discover his or her own angels, whatever they are.

30.

PERFECT PEACE

Peace, perfect peace, in this dark world of sin
(E. H. Bickersteth, 1825–1906)

The author of this hymn, Edward Henry Bickersteth, was vicar of Christ Church, Hampstead, when in August 1875 he went on holiday to Harrogate. On a Sunday morning he heard the vicar Canon Gibbon preach on the text, 'Thou wilt keep him in perfect peace, whose mind is stayed on thee' (Isa.26.3). As he rested after lunch that day he recalled the text and the sermon, and within a few minutes he composed the hymn.

Later that afternoon he went to visit an aged relative, Archdeacon Hill of Liverpool, whose life was nearing its end. He read the words of the hymn to the dying man and they gave him comfort. They have brought comfort and help to a vast multitude of people since that day.

1 The quality of peace

The hymn again and again speaks not merely of peace but of *perfect peace*. What sort of peace is that? What is its special quality? Where does it come from?

Edward Bickersteth – who later became Bishop of Exeter – recalled that the preacher that Sunday morning had pointed out that in the Hebrew the words of the text read 'Thou wilt keep him in peace, peace'. The repetition of the word *peace* was for the sake of emphasis. It indicated peace of a distinctive character, peace of a superlative kind, nothing less than the peace of God which passes all human understanding. It is with *that* peace that the hymn is concerned.

Now the question arises, Can this divine peace possibly be ours? And the hymn sets out to provide the answer to that question. In fact, the hymn as a whole consists of a series of questions and answers. The first line of each stanza (apart from the last) is a question about peace. The questions are all of a challenging nature, reminding us that there are many things in life that threaten our enjoyment of God's perfect peace. The second line supplies the answer to the questions asked, answers which are clear and reassuring.

Let us look at them in turn – the questions and the answers.

2 The enemies of peace

Edward Bickersteth, who belonged to the Evangelical school in the Church, recognized that the first and greatest enemy of peace is the evil in the world. So he begins by asking,

> Peace, perfect peace, in this dark world of sin?

Certainly sin is public enemy number one. It darkens the whole of life: the life of the world in general, the life of each one of us as individuals. It separates us one from another. It divides nation from nation. Worst of all, it alienates us from God in his holiness. Is reconciliation possible? The answer lies in the cross:

> The blood of Jesus whispers peace within –

that is, within our hearts. The hymn rightly points us to Calvary. Jesus made peace by the shedding of his blood on the cross (Col.1.20). So perfect peace may be ours: the peace of sins forgiven, the peace of unbroken fellowship with the Father.

But what about the pressures of everyday life, the multitudinous tasks to be fulfilled? We are such busy people! Our days are so over-crowded! Can we find God's perfect peace when by 'thronging duties pressed'? The answer is:

> To do the will of Jesus, this is rest.

It is not merely *what* we do but *why* we do it that matters. To seek in all our tasks to serve the Lord, to recollect his presence and to do everything in his name, is to know inner peace even on the busiest day.

Next, can we find that same peace 'with sorrows surging round'? No life is free from sorrows, our own and other people's. The answer to the question is:

On Jesus' bosom nought but calm is found.

The language is poetical and archaic, but the meaning is clear. To put it quite simply, we find peace and consolation in time of sorrow by keeping close to Jesus and resting in his love.

Anxiety about our 'loved ones' is another threat to our peace, whether in fact they are 'far away' or near at hand. We are often and rightly concerned about their safety and welfare and are inclined to worry. What then? We are to remember this:

In Jesus' keeping we are safe, and they.

Instead of worrying we must quietly commit them, as we commit ourselves, into the Lord's hands, assured that distance cannot separate them from *his* love any more than it does from ours.

Another question: what about 'the future', that future 'all unknown' to us? This is a pertinent question when we come to the crossroads of life. The way ahead is dark and uncertain. We don't know where to turn. But courage!

Jesus we know, and he is on the throne.

Here our peace lies in recognizing the lordship of Jesus and committing the unknown future to his direction.

The final question is about the final enemy that confronts us: 'death shadowing us and ours'. Is not death something to be feared? Can we face it with tranquillity? The answer to both questions is decisive:

121

Jesus has vanquished death and all its powers.

While we recognize the reality of death, we also know the reality of the risen Lord and his glorious Easter victory.

3 The secret of peace

The questions we have looked at are many and varied; but in a sense the answer to them all is the same. In a word, the answer is *Jesus*. Look at the stanzas again and you will notice that he is the key to every issue raised, whether it be life or death, sin or sorrow, the present or the future.

Perhaps the chief value of this hymn is that it consistently points us away from ourselves to our Lord. He himself is our peace, the ultimate secret of it all. 'Peace I leave with you,' he said, 'my own peace I give you. Let not your hearts be troubled and do not be afraid' (John 14.27).

But there is another secret, this time on the human level – and that is *faith*. The text in Isaiah which inspired the hymn says, 'Thou wilt keep him in perfect peace, whose mind is stayed on thee, *because he trusteth in thee*.' By such trust Jesus – all that he is and all that he has done for us – becomes real to us as our Saviour and Lord. However insecure we may be in ourselves, we are secure in him and shall remain so, till he calls us at last to 'heaven's perfect peace'.

31.

OUR DAILY WORK

Forth in thy name, O Lord, I go
(Charles Wesley, 1707–88)

This is not, in the usual sense, a morning hymn. It is a hymn about our daily work, the work to which we go forth at the beginning of the day. There are very few hymns which deal directly with the theme, and this one by the prince of English hymn-writers is all the more welcome. As we should expect, Wesley tackles it in a thoroughly Christian and biblical way.

Work is a very important subject, much in the news these days. Vast numbers of people, through no fault of their own, are without work. Others, through redundancy, find themselves deprived of the work they had. Yet others, of their own free will, choose to take strike action and abstain from work waiting to be done. But mercifully the great majority of men and women do have work, and if they are Christians this hymn has something very positive to say to them. When Wesley published it in 1739 he headed it, 'For believers before work'. It answers the question, In what spirit are we to face our daily work? And again, What difference does it make to our daily work if we are 'believers'?

1 Recognizing God in our work

The first thing to do is to get rid of the idea that our work is quite separate from our religion. We must never put worship and work in separate compartments, as though worship belongs to Sundays, work to weekdays – or as though the one is a spiritual and the other a secular activity. This is nonsense.

Work is an integral element in God's purpose for man's life. It is not a curse but a blessing. God himself is the supreme worker, the creator of heaven and earth. We ourselves, made in his image, have the creative instinct and find fulfilment in work. Christ as the village carpenter sanctified work and taught that the labourer is worthy of his hire.

Against this background we must interpret Wesley's hymn and make its prayer our own.

> Forth in thy name, O Lord, I go,
> My daily labour to pursue;
> Thee, only thee, resolved to know,
> In all I think, or speak, or do.

This is a prayer for an ordinary working day. The task before us is just the usual one – 'my daily labour to pursue'. But there is something that adds distinction to the task. We face it in the name of the Lord and that makes a vast difference. However mundane it may be, it is not just an irksome job to be done. It is part of our Christian service. As the second stanza says, it is the task that God in his wisdom has assigned to us. Hence our firm resolve to 'know' or acknowledge him – and him alone – not only in what we *do* but also in what we *think* and *say*.

2 Keeping faith with God in our work

Work of every kind has its peculiar temptations and pitfalls. The Christian believer should be aware of that fact and strive to keep faith with God in his work. Wesley recognized the necessity for this in a stanza of his hymn which is missing from most books:

> Preserve me from my calling's snare,
> And hide my simple heart above,
> Above the thorns of choking care,
> The gilded baits of worldly love.

Our different callings have their different snares. We pray that we may be shielded from them, and lifted above them, whatever they may be. Two are here singled out by way of illustration. First, 'the thorns of choking care' – that is, over-anxiety, business worries. Those in positions of responsibility will be well aware of this danger. Burdensome care not only robs us of God's peace but chokes our spiritual life. The other snare is money, which is evidently what Wesley meant by 'the gilded baits of worldly love'. Love of the world and love of money go together. They are a form of idolatry which inevitably rivals the love of God and in the end displaces it.

In our workaday lives we must guard against these temptations and keep faith with God. Above all we must maintain our loyalty to Christ, be vigilant and prayerful, and not become absorbed in the passing things of time. So we pray:

> Give me to bear thy easy yoke,
>   And every moment watch and pray;
> And still to things eternal look,
>   And hasten to thy glorious day.

3 Glorifying God in our work

All this means that in our work, as much as in our worship, we must remember God's presence and seek his glory.

> Thee may I set at my right hand,
>   Whose eyes my inmost substance see,
> And labour on at thy command,
>   And offer all my works to thee.

Nothing is hidden from God. 'Everything lies naked and exposed to the eyes of the one with whom we have to reckon' (Heb.4.13). So it is with our work. We must do it as in *his* sight and for his acceptance. St Paul urged the Christian slaves of his day to fulfil their tasks 'not with eyeservice, as men pleasers,

but with sincerity of heart and reverence for the Lord.' And he
added: 'Whatever you do, work at it with all your heart, as
working for the Lord, not for men. . . . It is the Lord you are
serving' (Col.3.22–24).

Charles Wesley reflects this teaching in his final stanza:

> For thee delightfully employ
>   Whate'er thy bounteous grace hath given;
> And run my course with even joy,
>   And closely walk with thee to heaven.

Our work is not to be a drudgery. We are to take delight in
employing the talents, skills and faculties which God in his
'bounteous grace' has given us. It is this that imparts to life a
sense of fulfilment.

Happy are those who can find such fulfilment in their daily
work. Unhappily not all are in that position. Many are
compelled to do jobs which leave them unfulfilled, unsatisfied.
Fulfilment in such cases must be sought in other directions,
outside one's regular employment, while ultimate fulfilment
must wait for the life to come. Perhaps this is why Wesley
concludes his hymn in the way he does. Nothing is perfect here
below. Life has many disappointments and frustrations. Meanwhile we must patiently run our course with 'even joy' –
meaning joy that is constant, not up-and-down – and closely
walk with the Lord to heaven. Could we have a better
companion on the road? And could there be a better end to our
pilgrimage?

32.

LIFE – A DOXOLOGY

Fill thou my life, O Lord my God
(H. Bonar, 1808–89)

Horatius Bonar was one of the leading figures in the Scottish Church during the last century. Born in Edinburgh and educated at the university, he exercised a powerful ministry for many years at the Chalmers Memorial Church in that city. He was a man of many gifts and seemingly boundless energy and won renown as a scholar, preacher and author.

Today he is chiefly remembered by his hymns. He is rightly regarded as the prince of Scottish hymn-writers. Among his best known hymns are 'I heard the voice of Jesus say', and 'Here, O my Lord, I see thee face to face'; but perhaps none is finer than this hymn, 'Fill thou my life, O Lord my God'.

1 Life's praise

When he published the hymn in his *Hymns of Faith and Love*, 1867, Dr Bonar headed it 'Life's Praise'. This indeed is the keynote of the entire hymn (it was originally twice as long). The theme running through it is that the whole of life should be a doxology. Hence it begins:

> Fill thou my life, O Lord my God,
>   In every part with praise,
> That my whole being may proclaim
>   Thy being and thy ways.

Bonar's own life, especially his later life, became a commentary on these words. At the beginning of his ministry he was known to be a somewhat hard and intolerant sort of person. His narrow Calvinistic creed and stern doctrinal preaching made him a man to be feared rather than loved. But gradually over the years, as he drew closer to Christ and sensed more deeply the love of God, he changed. His character mellowed, his sympathies broadened, and his life radiated a spirit of joy and gratitude. He came to see that Christianity was not just a matter of correct beliefs and sound words. It had to express itself in daily life and conduct. And this was also true, he saw, of Christian praise:

> Not for the lip of praise alone,
>   Nor e'en the praising heart,
> I ask, but for a life made up
>   Of praise in every part.

This stanza brings together the three great agencies of praise. In doing so it echoes the prayer at the end of the General Thanksgiving in the BCP: 'We beseech thee, give us that due sense of all thy mercies, that our *hearts* may be unfeignedly thankful, and that we show forth thy praise, not only with our *lips*, but in our *lives*, by giving up ourselves to thy service. . . .' In reference to those words Bishop Taylor Smith used to say that while thanksgiving is good, thanksliving is better.

2 Life's common things

We are inclined to associate praise – primarily if not exclusively – with church-going, hymn-singing and the like. But praise is not just a religious activity. It has a place in our ordinary, everyday affairs. Bonar recognized this when he wrote:

> Praise in the common things of life,
>   Its goings out and in,
> Praise in each duty and each deed,
>   However small and mean.

And the lines which immediately follow in the original work speak of praise in 'the common words' we speak and in 'life's common looks and tones'; and likewise in the life we share at home with those we love.

For many of us the home is the most difficult place in which to show forth God's praise. It is the place where we are best known and where we reveal most clearly the manner of people we are. Doubtless we are better Christians at church than at home! But Sunday religion is not enough. For the believer every day is holy. And so is every place, as Bonar stresses in a stanza omitted from our hymn books:

> Not in the temple-crowd alone,
> Where holy voices chime,
> But in the silent paths of earth,
> The quiet rooms of time.

It is a point worth remembering that we can praise God in silence as well as in song, in solitude as well as in company, in the quiet of the home as well as in the sanctuary. This doubtless is what is meant by 'praise in the common things of life'. And this is what St Paul meant when he told us to do *everything* to the glory of God, including even what we eat or drink (1 Cor.10.31).

3 Life's hallowing

The prince of Scottish hymn-writers has something else to teach us. Praise, like prayer, hallows the life of the Christian – the whole life. We are inclined to draw a false distinction between the sacred and the secular, whereas true sanctity pervades every aspect of life, the entire personality, every moment of time. As Bonar wrote:

> So shall no part of day or night
> From sacredness be free,

But all my life, in every step,
Be fellowship with thee.

Is this an impossible ideal, beyond our realization? Perhaps it is. But surely it is a good thing to cherish high ideals in the spiritual life. We shall not achieve perfection now. We know that. But we must not be content with the second rate, the second best. Jesus said, 'Be perfect, as your heavenly Father is perfect' (Matt.5.48). *That* is the standard we are to aim at. Let us set our sights high. Let us endeavour to make the whole of life an act of praise and in doing so consecrate all its activities to the greater glory of God.

So shalt thou, Lord, from me, e'en me,
Receive the glory due,
And so shall I begin on earth
The song for ever new.

33.

DEATH

Lord, it belongs not to my care
(Richard Baxter, 1615–91)

This is a hymn about death: a sombre subject indeed, but an unavoidable one. For death is a universal fact. It is the one absolute certainty in this uncertain world. We may try to forget it, ignore it, dismiss it, but in the end we cannot escape it. Surely then the more sensible and realistic attitude is to face it; and as Christians there is no reason why we should not face it without embarrassment or fear.

This is what Richard Baxter, the seventeenth century Puritan divine, is doing in his hymn, first published in 1681. It is based on some words St Paul wrote to the Christians at Philippi. In his imprisonment awaiting trial, he is surveying his prospects: will the issue be life or death? And he finds himself in a dilemma, torn between the two. 'For to me to live is Christ and to die is gain,' he writes. 'Yet what shall I choose? I do not know! My personal desire is to depart and be with Christ, for that is far better; but for *your* sake it is more necessary that I should continue to live on in the body' (Phil.1.21–24).

Here in this passage are the themes dealt with in the hymn: life in the present, life in the world to come, and what lies between – death. Let us think on these things.

1 Our present life

Baxter is pondering the same issues that confronted the apostle when he writes:

> Lord, it belongs not to my care
>   Whether I die or live;
> To love and serve thee is my share,
>   And this thy grace must give.

The issue does not rest with him; it is in higher hands. His 'care' or concern is not whether he lives or dies. What matters for him is that, come what may, he may remain faithful to the Lord and continue to love and serve him. And for this, he acknowledges, he is wholly dependent on the grace of God. Here is the language of a man of strong faith who having fully committed his life to God leaves the future in his hands. So he continues:

> If life be long, I will be glad,
>   That I may long obey;
> If short, yet why should I be sad
>   To end my little day?

If life be long? Or if it be short? Consideration is given to each in turn. But in facing these questions let us be clear that the value of human life is not measured in terms of years but in terms of achievement. Many a long life has accomplished very little. Many a short one has done an immense amount of good and left behind a rich legacy. As Baxter sees it, the advantage of a long life is that it enables a person to serve the Lord for a long time. We should view life in the same way. 'To love and serve thee is my share', whether life be long *or* short. We are here in this world not to be ornamental but to be useful.

2 Our approaching death

Death lies ahead of us all. To remember that, and to think about it from time to time, is a sober and sensible exercise. It has a bearing on the way we live. It helps us to get our priorities right and to ask, 'Am I making the best use of my life? Am I putting the best into it?' If we never seriously consider such questions we may not be ready for death when it comes.

How are we to face it? The hymn gives this assurance:

> Christ leads me through no darker rooms
> Than he went through before;
> He that unto God's kingdom comes
> Must enter by this door.

Death is a door. It is not so much an end as an entrance: the end indeed of our earthly existence but the entrance into the life of heaven. There is no other way into *that* life except through death. And Jesus himself has trod that way before us. This is our great comfort. In making himself one with us, our Lord faced not only life but death – and what lies beyond death. That is the significance of the words in the creed, 'He descended into hell'. The word 'hell' here is *hades* and simply means the unseen world, the place of departed spirits. In dying Jesus shared our lot to the full. As Bishop Westcott put it, 'He hallowed every condition of human existence. We cannot be where he has not been.'

That being so, we can approach death with confidence. If we have trusted Christ with our life we can surely trust him with our death as well, knowing that the door through which we shall then pass will usher us into the presence of our Lord. This then is our prayer:

> Come, Lord, when grace hath made me meet
>> Thy blessed face to see;
> For if thy work on earth be sweet,
>> What will thy glory be!

3 Our final destiny

We are thus led by the aid of this hymn to think of our final destiny – heaven. And how gloriously different will the life of heaven be from that of earth! Richard Baxter felt this strongly when he wrote:

> Then shall I end my sad complaints
>> And weary, sinful days,
> And join with the triumphant saints
>> That sing my Saviour's praise.

We can understand Baxter's feelings. He lived in troublous times; he suffered much ill health; he lost his beloved wife after a long, painful illness. But his chief sorrow came after the Civil War when, because he refused to conform to the Church of England, he was subject to bitter persecution and sentenced by the notorious Judge Jeffreys to imprisonment. Small wonder that for him the prospect of heaven and 'The Saints' Everlasting Rest' (the title of a popular book he wrote) was an alluring one. In the heavenly city there will be no death or mourning, no more crying or pain. God will wipe away every tear and make all things new.

That is one aspect of heaven we can speak of with certainty.
The Bible gives us other glimpses too. Yet in the end we are
bound to acknowledge that we know very little about heaven,
and Baxter realized this too:

> My knowledge of that life is small,
>   The eye of faith is dim;
> But 'tis enough that Christ knows all,
>   And I shall be with him.

It doesn't matter much that *we* know little of heaven. The
important thing is that Christ knows all – and more important
still that there we shall be with him. That is why the apostle
declared that while to *live* is Christ, to *die* is gain, for to die is to
be with Christ. And that, he said, is 'far, far better'. For the
believer both life and death are good. Life is good because
Christ is with us. Death is better because we shall be with him.

34.

HEAVEN

Jerusalem the golden
(Bernard of Cluny, 12th cent., tr. J. M. Neale, 1818–66)

Two things may be said by way of introduction about this
ancient hymn. The first concerns its author, Bernard of Cluny
(not to be confused with his famous contemporary, St Bernard
of Clairvaux). His exact dates are not known, but he belonged to
the twelfth century. Early in life he became a monk and entered
the great abbey of Cluny in France – the largest, wealthiest and
most powerful religious establishment of its day. There Bernard remained until his death.

The second thing concerns his poem from which the hymn is derived. It is an extraordinary work, very long and involved, entitled *De Contemptu Mundi* ('On Contempt of the World'). In general it is a burning and outspoken invective against the wickedness and depravity of the world. And by the 'world' Bernard meant not merely society at large but the religious world as well, the world he encountered within his own monastic life. The greater part of the poem is taken up with this theme. But that is not our present concern. Intermingled with the terrifying pictures of the gross evils of the age are – by way of contrast – glowing visions of the glories of heaven; and it is from these portions that John Mason Neale (1818–66) made his translation. He divided it into four separate hymns, of which 'Jerusalem the golden' is by far the best known.

1 Thinking about heaven

This then is a hymn about heaven, the new Jerusalem of the Apocalypse:

> Jerusalem the golden,
>   With milk and honey blest,
> Beneath thy contemplation
>   Sink heart and voice opprest.

Note that line 'Beneath thy *contemplation*'. Heaven is a subject we are invited to contemplate: that is, to consider, to think about, to meditate on. How often do we do that? Modern Christians are not inclined or encouraged to think about heaven a great deal – certainly not so much as those of the past. The hymn book illustrates this. The typical Victorian hymn was not complete without making a final reference to the life to come.

This trend has now been reversed. Modern hymns do not have much to say about heaven. As Christians we are much more earthly-minded and tend to concentrate on the duties and responsibilities of the present life. That, of course, is good to a certain extent, but in the process we have lost something of supreme value. Some years ago D. R. Davies wrote a book called *The World we have Forgotten*. It was a book about heaven. We cannot afford to forget that other world. Heaven is the goal of our pilgrimage, the ultimate fulfilment of God's purpose for our lives. To lose sight of it is to diminish the gospel and distort our spiritual vision.

One value of this hymn and others like it is that it lifts us above our mundane existence, the purely human and materialistic things of life. It helps us with 'heart and voice opprest' – that is, quietened, humbled, subdued – to contemplate the glory to come, the good things which God has prepared for those who love him.

2 Portraying heaven

But how are we to think of heaven? What do we know about it? Not very much, in fact, as the hymn honestly acknowledges:

> I know not, O I know not,
>   What social joys are there,
> What radiancy of glory,
>   What light beyond compare.

Heaven is entirely different from this life; and since it lies outside our present experience, it is also beyond our human comprehension. It can only be depicted to us in symbolical, pictorial language, as is done in the book of Revelation. Bernard freely makes use of this language in his hymn. Heaven is portrayed as 'the holy city, new Jerusalem', in accordance with St John's vision. To the Jews Jerusalem was the *holy* city because it was regarded as God's chosen dwelling place. Heaven is the genuine holy city because God is truly there.

The hymn provides other pictures. It tells us that heaven is *beautiful* and speaks of its 'radiancy of glory'. It is 'golden' because John saw that the city was pure gold, its walls built of jasper, its foundations adorned with precious jewels (Rev.21.18–20). All such language simply means, as another part of the hymn puts it, that heaven is 'the Land of Beauty' where 'all things of beauty meet'.

Again, heaven is *sociable*. It must be so, for God made us for one another as well as for himself. We cannot find fulfilment in solitude, only in fellowship. Thus it is with the citizens of the new Jerusalem:

> There is the throne of David,
> And there, from care released,
> The song of them that triumph,
> The shout of them that feast.

Heaven is something like a glorious family reunion, with all its members at home with one another and with the Lord. Heaven is the communion of saints in its final perfection.

Once more, heaven is *musical*. In heaven everyone is singing, angels and archangels along with redeemed mankind:

> They stand, those halls of Zion,
> Conjubilant with song. . .

In the Bible, declared Erik Routley, heaven resembles a great choral society. Its music is symbolic of its pure, unalloyed joy. There will be no sorrow in heaven. God will wipe away all tears.

3 Preparing for heaven

How are we to prepare for heaven? By way of answer let us not forget that heaven, the life of the spirit, does not altogether lie in the future. It starts on earth. Here already, so to speak, we have the first instalment. As a modern hymn puts it, '*Now* is eternal life'! So Canon Paterson Smyth wrote, 'It is not so much that we have to go to heaven: heaven has to come to us first. Heaven has to begin in ourselves.'

This means that we best prepare for heaven by cultivating our inner, spiritual life: by deepening our communion with God through Christ day by day. The whole of life is a preparation for heaven. And if we do so prepare we can look forward to heaven with genuine longing and expectancy. Our hymn ends on that note in its original version:

> O sweet and blessèd country,
>   Shall I ever see thy face?
> O sweet and blessèd country,
>   Shall I ever win thy grace?

Those questions receive a triumphant answer in Dr Neale's original translation:

> Exult, O dust and ashes!
>   The Lord shall be thy part;
> His only, his for ever,
>   Thou shalt be, and thou art!

This is a splendid note on which to finish the hymn. Dust and ashes we may be, as far as our bodies are concerned. But we are more than that, far more than that on the spiritual level. We are the Lord's own eternal possession – 'His only, his for ever'. And we are this now. That being so, our life in this world is not only a preparation for heaven. It is also a foretaste of it.

INDEX

INDEX OF HYMNS

Other Mowbray Sermon Outlines
Series Editor: D. W. Cleverley Ford